MA
REPAIR KIT

LIZ & SUE ATKINSON
TIM SCOTT

Illustrated by David Farris

Hodder
Children's
Books

a division of Hodder Headline plc

Text copyright © 1999 Liz & Sue Atkinson and Tim Scott

Illustrations copyright © 1999 David Farris

Cover illustration by Mark Duffin

Published by Hodder Children's Books 1999

ISBN 0 340 64679 9

A Catalogue record for this book is available from the British Library.

Printed by The Guernsey Press Company Limited,Guernsey,C.I

Hodder Children's Books
A division of Hodder Headline plc
338 Euston Road
London NW1 3BH

CONTENTS

For all the children over the years who have said
to us, "I can't do maths, Miss."
S.A. and L.A.

Dedicated to my nephews and nieces,
Alfie, Gus, Hannah, Ivan, Jacob and Olive.
And to Chancellors of the Exchequer everywhere.
T.S.

INTRODUCTION

The big question: why bother?

Wherever you are, whatever you're doing – at some stage in life you'll need maths. That's the way the world works.

You've got a point.

Of course, there are people who will go around telling you all sorts of whopping great lies about maths.

WHOPPING GREAT LIE NUMBER ONE

Don't bother. You'll never need to use maths.

You can use a calculator anyway. It's not worth learning.

ALERT! ALERT!

These people are trying to get you to have a rubbish life. Because without maths your life will be a struggle.

Rubbish Life | Not Rubbish Life

I mean, as you go through life what are people going to think if you can't do maths?

Even a fool can see you'll need some simple maths in life.

I guess he just wanted to have a rubbish life. I'll help him on his way.

Hmm. He can't do maths.

TEACHER   **EMPLOYER**   **GIRLFRIEND**

Of course you need maths! You need maths for all sorts of day to day things. You need it for measuring, for playing games, and what about when you use money? Are you just going to guess? Look, say you want to buy a skateboard for £42.29.

Here it is.

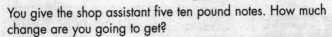

You give the shop assistant five ten pound notes. How much change are you going to get?

Are you really going to get out a calculator? Doesn't that frankly make you look a bit silly? And what happens when you forget the calculator? I mean you might as well just get out a great big sign with flashing lights saying: 'I feel stupid now'.

And there are other examples from all areas of real life. For example – this definitely happened on live television, and we're not just making it up:

One hundred and forty-seven. No – forty-six. Hang on – thirty-six plus . . . er . . . hang on. Oh dear – I feel stupid now.

And this really happened to a couple on holiday, honestly:

I could do with a hat like that for the office. 3,000 pesetas. How much is that in pounds . . . two . . . two hundred – maybe it's two thousand?

I FEEL STUPID!

He can't work it out!

3 000 pesetas

OK – so much for Whopping Great Lie Number One. So let's move on to . . .

WHOPPING GREAT LIE NUMBER TWO

Oh – maths – yeah – maths is really hard.

You won't be able to do maths. Maths is for clever people.

When someone says this to you, immediately picture them standing in this:

INTRODUCTION

Because what they have told you is a huge pile of stinking rubbish. Anyone can do maths. For example – you! Yes – you. No – not the person over there – You!

And this book is going to show you how it's not so difficult after all. And you won't be on your own either. Oh no. There'll be some friends to help you along every step of the way. Meet the mechanics at the Repair Kit garage.

Here's Zelda. Say hello to everyone, Zelda.

> Hi there. Welcome to the garage. It's a cool place.

Say hello (dull) Colin.

> Hello. I'm a bit dull so I've sharpened all my pencils and put them in my top pocket to liven myself up. I'm very good at summarising things in a clear way though.

Yes – thanks Colin. And here's Steven The Stupid Monster. Say hello, Steven.

> Hello, my name's . . . what was it again?

It's Steven, Steven. There'll also be a few other people who we'll introduce along the way. Say hello, team.

> Hello.

> Hello.

> Hello.

Now, before we get stuck in, we need to make sure we've got a few things.

You'll find it useful to have all the following – except one. Guess which one you won't need as we make our way through the book.

Clue: it's this one.

It's the moose. You won't need a moose but you will need the other things, so if you've rushed out and got a moose – you'd better go and take it back . . . eh, Steven?

Any words that are difficult to understand are in the back. I've put a pair of my glasses under tricky words – like this – ADDITION.

You'll find I've explained them all in the back in 'Colin's Glasses Glossary' on page 134.

Good idea, Colin.

And when you see this sign it means you mustn't use a calculator.

Thanks, Zelda. OK. I think we can get started now.

Getting Good at
Adding and Subtracting

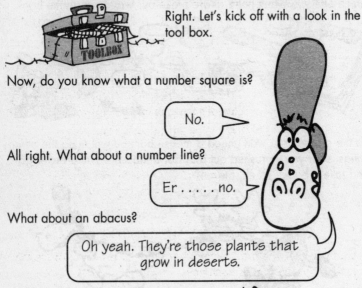

Right. Let's kick off with a look in the tool box.

Now, do you know what a number square is?

No.

All right. What about a number line?

Er . . . . . no.

What about an abacus?

Oh yeah. They're those plants that grow in deserts.

Right, I think you are thinking of a cactus there, Steven, which looks like this:

whereas an abacus looks like this:

Never mind, we'll explain what an abacus, a number line and a number square are in a minute. They're all useful tools to make it easy to get the right answer.

And here to guide you is Superfrog who leaps down the number line . . .

. . . and here's Horace the Puffin who hops about the number square.

Hi there!

Right, let's start with . . .

Easy thing to do: adding and subtracting 10

Here's a number square. It goes up to a
hundred so it's called . . . yes . . .
a hundred square.

6 + 10 = 16

16 + 10 = 26

26 + 10 = 36

1	2	3	4	5	6	7	8	9	10
11	12	13	14	15	16	17	18	19	20
21	22	23	24	25	26	27	28	29	30
31	32	33	34	35	36	37	38	39	40
41	42	43	44	45	46	47	48	49	50
51	52	53	54	55	56	57	58	59	60
61	62	63	64	65	66	67	68	69	70
71	72	73	74	75	76	77	78	79	80
81	82	83	84	85	86	87	88	89	90
91	92	93	94	95	96	97	98	99	100

Can you see what's happening? Adding 10 is easy. Horace the
Puffin hops 10 spaces each time.

You try this one:

36 + 10 =

Subtracting 10 is easy too. Just go back the other way. Look at
Horace the Puffin hopping back 10 spaces.

1	2	3	4	5	6	7	8	9	10
11	12	13	14	15	16	17	18	19	20
21	22	23	24	25	26	27	28	29	30
31	32	33	34	35	36	37	38	39	40
41	42	43	44	45	46	47	48	49	50
51	52	53	54	55	56	57	58	59	60
61	62	63	64	65	66	67	68	69	70
71	72	73	74	75	76	77	78	79	80
81	82	83	84	85	86	87	88	89	90
91	92	93	94	95	96	97	98	99	100

94 – 10 = 84

84 – 10 = 74

Now you try this one: 74 – 10 =

ADDING AND SUBTRACTING

SUPERFROG'S NUMBER LINE

When you add on a number line, you go this way.

When you subtract you go the other way.

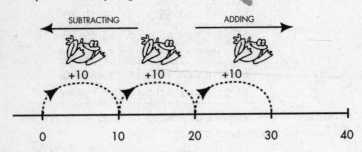

This number line shows Superfrog hopping 10 at a time.

Try these:

1. Superfrog is leaping in 10s from 7.

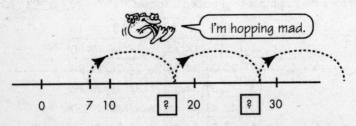

She lands on 7, 17, 27, 37 . . . Write the other numbers in your notebook up to 100.

You can use the hundred square on page 7 to help you.

Adding 10 to any number up to 100 is easy. Try this:

2.   13 + 10 =

Here is that sum on an abacus with the tens and units.

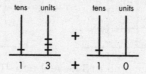

3.   39 + 10 =

Here it is as tens and units on an abacus.

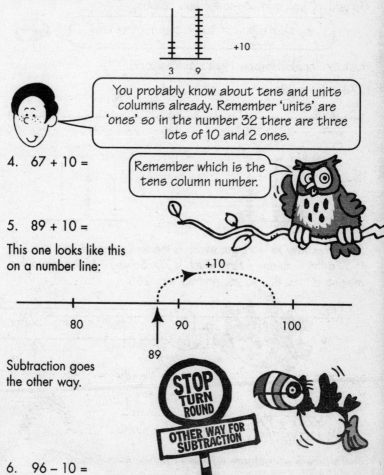

+10

You probably know about tens and units columns already. Remember 'units' are 'ones' so in the number 32 there are three lots of 10 and 2 ones.

4.   67 + 10 =

Remember which is the tens column number.

5.   89 + 10 =

This one looks like this on a number line:

+10

80   89   90   100

Subtraction goes the other way.

STOP
TURN
ROUND

OTHER WAY FOR
SUBTRACTION

6.   96 − 10 =

9

ADDING AND SUBTRACTING

The good news is that adding 10 is just as easy with much larger numbers.

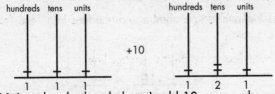

Here is 111 (one hundred and eleven) add 10, on an abacus.

The answer is 121 (one hundred and twenty-one).

To add 10 you add one to the tens column.

> Or take a hop of 10 on the number line!

Exactly. Thanks Horace. Here's another one.

$276 + 10 = 286$

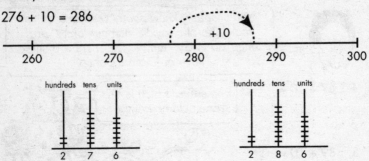

See? You have to work out which is the tens column in the number. In 276 the 7 means 7 tens which is 70. So you add the ten to that making 8 tens, 80, so you end up with 286.

Try these.

> Decide which is the tens column first.

1. $365 + 10 =$
2. $3,234 + 10 =$
3. $56,789 + 10 =$
4. $123,456,789 + 10 =$

There's more about large numbers and using an abacus in the chapter about place value.

OK, now if you can add on 10, you can easily add 9 . . .

More easy things to do: adding and subtracting 9

If you want to add 9 to a number, you can add 10 first. That's easy. Then take 1 away.

This is what it looks like on the number line.

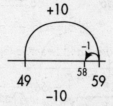

49 + 10 is 59. So, 49 + 9 is 1 less than 59 = 58

Try these in your notebook or in your head. Do them by first adding 10 and then going back 1.

1. 23 + 9 =
2. 52 + 9 =
3. 67 + 9 =
4. 89 + 9 =

Do you remember that subtracting 10 was just the reverse of adding 10? Look back to the pattern on the hundred square on page 7.

So, subtracting 9 can be done by subtracting 10 first, then adding 1. Say we want to do 72 − 9.

Start with 72 − 10 which is 62. But leaping 10 was too far, we only wanted to take away 9, so we have to leap back the other way just one number.

72 − 9 is 63.

Don't forget to add the 1.

−10

60 62 63   70 72

11

ADDING AND SUBTRACTING

The good news is that not only can you use adding 10 to add or take away 9, but you can use it to add or take away 11.

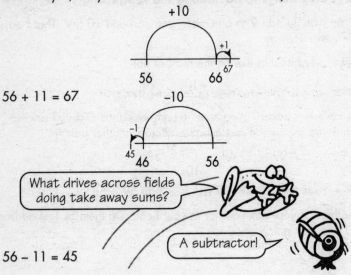

$56 + 11 = 67$

$56 - 11 = 45$

What drives across fields doing take away sums?

A subtractor!

See? You do the same thing. Do the 10 first, then another little hop of 1. That makes it easy.

Always make calculations easier when you can.

Another easy thing: numbers ending in zero are easy to add

Adding 20 or 30 or 40 or any other multiple of 10 is easy.

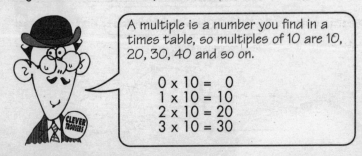

A multiple is a number you find in a times table, so multiples of 10 are 10, 20, 30, 40 and so on.

$0 \times 10 = 0$
$1 \times 10 = 10$
$2 \times 10 = 20$
$3 \times 10 = 30$

You know 16 + 10 is 26 so 16 + 20 = 36 and 16 + 30 is 46. Try these ones in your head or your notebook.

1. 16 + 50 =
2. 36 + 20 =
3. 36 + 50 =
4. 36 + 60 =

Another easy thing: looking for number patterns

If you can see a pattern in numbers it can help a lot. Did you see the pattern in the answers to the last quiz? Here's another pattern.

$$19 + 10 = 29$$
$$19 + 11 = 30$$
$$19 + 12 = 31$$
$$19 + 13 = 32$$
$$19 + 14 = 33$$

Have a go at these three questions and then guess what the next numbers in the pattern are.

5. 21 + 16 =
6. 22 + 17 =
7. 23 + 18 =

Carry on in your note book up to 45. Your answers should all be odd numbers.

When you can't share numbers out equally between two people, numbers are odd. So 5 biscuits between 2 people has 1 left over, so 5 is an odd number. The pattern for odd numbers is 1, 3, 5, 7, 9, 11, 13, 15 and so on.

Another easy thing: putting the larger number first is easiest

Look at this. 9 + 35 looks quite hard.

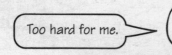

Too hard for me.

13

ADDING AND SUBTRACTING

But look Steven – it's much easier if you turn it around and think of
35 + 9 =

Try these in your head. Turn them around to make them easier.

1. 2 + 17 =
2. 4 + 76 =
3. 2 + 45 =

More easy things to do: adding 19, 29, 39

Now something very clever. Remember how you can add 9 to any
number by adding 10 first and taking 1 away? Well, you can also
add 19 like that. You start by adding 20 and take off 1. Adding
29 is easy too. Just do it like this:

17 + 29 = 46

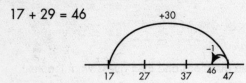

Try the ones below.

> Remember to do an easy addition first,
> and don't forget to check what you do.

Draw a number line like this if you want or make a picture of it in
your head.

20   30   40   50   60   70

4. 9 + 25

CLUE:
Do 25 + 10
and take off
the 1

I've found a clue!

5. 23 + 19
6. 34 + 29

14

Use what you already know.

If you are one of those people who tell themselves that they are hopeless at maths you might find that you already know lots more than you think you do. If you know some easy adding and taking away, you can use that to work out much harder sums. Look, if you know that 3 + 3 is 6, you can work out that 30 + 30 is 60 and 300 + 300 is 600.

So what is 3,000,000 (three million) add 3,000,000?

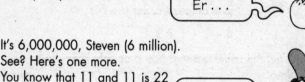

Er...

It's 6,000,000, Steven (6 million).
See? Here's one more.
You know that 11 and 11 is 22
so what is 1,100 + 1,100?

Er...

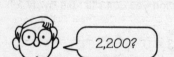

2,200?

Very good, Colin. You're not just a pretty face.

BE A WHIZZ AND DO THIS QUIZ

1. You can easily work out that 15 add 3 is 18.
   So what is 150 + 30?
2. You know 6 and 4 makes 10. So what is 600 add 400?

Here are some harder ones. No clues this time.

3. 70   + 30   =
4. 90   + 40   =
5. 800   + 103   =
6. 90   + 80   =
7. 6,000 + 10,000 =

ADDING AND SUBTRACTING

Do you still think you don't know anything about adding and taking away? You probably know more than you think you do. You'll need some facts.

> I thought it was healthier not to have fats and fried food.

Yes, facts Steven, not fats. Right.

If you are adding, you can add as many numbers as you want.
Try this one. 1 + 2 + 3 + 4 =

The answer is 10.

You can add numbers in any order and you still get the same answer. Try those same numbers in a different order like this:

4 + 2 + 1 + 3 =

See? You still get the same answer! You probably knew both those facts already.

With subtraction you can still take away lots of numbers:

6 − 1 − 2 − 3 = 0.

> But if you try to do this in a different order you won't get the same answer:

1 − 6 − 3 − 2 (The answer to this is minus 10.)

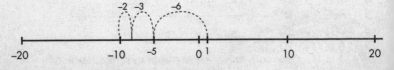

You can add any amount of numbers together in any order you want, but you can't do that with subtractions.

Thanks, Wise Owl. This is very important to help you to check your work. Look.

20 + 30 is 50. Now take off the 30 and you get back to 20 where you started.

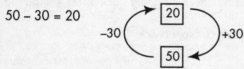

50 − 30 = 20

Try these 'round and rounds'.

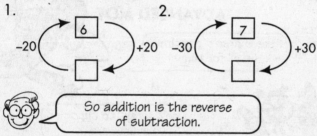

1.

−20   6   +20

2.

−30   7   +30

So addition is the reverse of subtraction.

Yes! And if you know that, you can follow our next wise rule.

Always check your calculations using the opposite operation.

An operation isn't a thing doctors do with knives in this case. +, −, x and ÷ are all called operations.

Yes, thank you, Mr. Clevertrousers. Now, try these:

17 + 3 is 20. How can you check this sum using subtraction?

ADDING AND SUBTRACTING

Try the number line. Start at 17, and hop on 3.

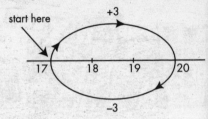

Now hop back 3 and get back to 17!

BASIC MOT! (MISERABLE OLD TEST)

Try to do these on a number line and check them using subtraction.

1. Start at 13 and add 5. Check by going back 5. Do you get back to 13?
2. Start at 21 and hop on 6. Now check.

And now . . . Impress your friends.

ADVANCED MOT

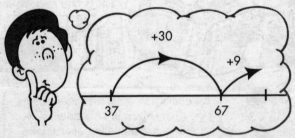

There aren't any clues at all for these!

Don't forget to check your answers.

Draw a number line in your notebook if you want, or make a picture of one in your mind.

1. 37 + 39   =
2. 41 + 49   =
3. 56 + 29   =

COLIN'S CHALKBOARD CONCLUSIONS

1. Always try to make calculations easier when you can.

2. Use what you already know.

3. You can add any amount of numbers together in any order you want, but you can't change the order with subtractions.

4. Always check your work using the opposite operation (so you can check a subtraction by doing an addition).

Aren't you supposed to be doing maths in your head – rather than on it, Steven?

Ohh.

What Teachers Don't Tell you About
Making Adding and Subtracting Even Easier

Do you want to make maths easier for yourself?

Oh boy . . . yes.

Good, because there are some things that teachers don't always tell you that can make things a lot easier. They're all in 'Colin's Box of Hints'.

Colin's Box of Hints

Right, now, if you know your 2 times table you can already double numbers to 10. Like this:

$1 \times 2 = 2$
$2 \times 2 = 4$

Multiplying 2 by 2 is exactly the same as doubling 2. Yes, it is — because $2 + 2 = 4$. Here's another.

$3 \times 2 = 6$

And this means the same as saying double 3 is 6. ($3 + 3 = 6$)

Exactly. Can you see how closely + and x are linked? I'm doubling and doing addition or multiplication. You see instead of multiplying by two – you can just double numbers instead, which is easier!

Right, time for . . .

THE GREAT DOUBLING QUIZ!

Here's Colin with his twin brother, Callum, to tell you how it works.

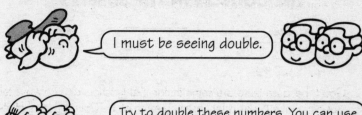

I must be seeing double.

Try to double these numbers. You can use the two times table or you can add!

1. 11
2. 20
3. 100
4. 30
5. 15
6. 24

Now multiply these numbers by 2.

7. 16 x 2 =
8. 200 x 2 =

Now add these.

9. 25 + 25 =
10. 45 + 45 =

Thanks, Colin and Callum. Do you see? You can double numbers by multiplying, or by adding. And you get the same answer.

It will really help you if you can learn all your doubles up to a hundred.

You can also use doubling as a very quick way to do some additions that are almost doubles. Have a go at these.

THE DOUBLES IN THE BUBBLES

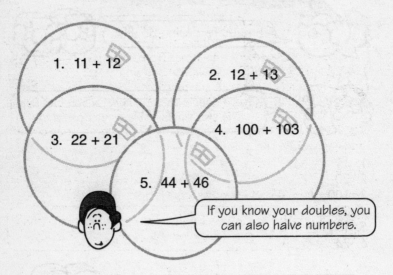

1. 11 + 12
2. 12 + 13
3. 22 + 21
4. 100 + 103
5. 44 + 46

If you know your doubles, you can also halve numbers.

Try this one. 100 − 49 =

Tricky? Well – you know that double 50 is 100. So 100 − 50 is 50, so take away 49 is one less, so the answer is 51.
Here's Superfrog to show you how that worked.

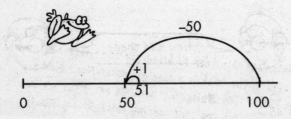

6. 80 − 39 =
7. 100 − 51 =
8. 66 − 32 =

Have a go at these. The answers are in the back if you get stuck.

Right, this is about changing the order of numbers.

Excuse me – waiter . . . I'd like to change my order from the salad to egg and chips please.

Yes, it's not numbers changing order like that, Steven. Look at this addition sum.

8 + 4 + 2 =

Now see how Wise Owl works it out.

To do this I'm going to first add the 8 and the 2 because I know that 8 + 2 is 10.

8 + 4 + 2

Then I'm going to add the 4 to make 14.

Ahh – they don't call you Wise Owl for nothing.

You're right – I have to pay them.

We interrupt this book to bring you some fantastic news! Included at the back is a free games section. Play a game called 'Ten Whispers'. Now. Go on. What are you waiting for? Are you still reading this? Go on. Now!!

Now – take a look at this sum: 26 + 34 + 24

Ohh – that looks hard.

Try changing the order of the numbers, Steven. Look.

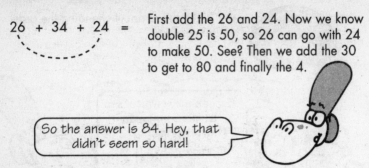

$26 + 34 + 24 =$

First add the 26 and 24. Now we know double 25 is 50, so 26 can go with 24 to make 50. See? Then we add the 30 to get to 80 and finally the 4.

So the answer is 84. Hey, that didn't seem so hard!

Very good, Steven. OK. Let's try this one. Can you see how to make it easy?

$16 + 78 + 4 =$

Pair 16 with 4 and get 20 and then add on the 78.

$20 + 78 = 98$

> If you didn't know that 16 and 4 is 20 you can always ask someone to play '20 Whispers' with you. It's on page 128.

Now see if you can find easy ways to do these sums (there are lots of different ways).

1. $5 + 17 + 5 + 3 =$

> For this, you could add the 5 and 5 to get 10 and then the 17 and 3 to make 20, then 10 + 20 is 30.

Nice one, Zelda. How about this?

2. $45 + 20 + 5 + 30 =$

> On this one you could add the 45 and the 5 to make 50 then add the 20 and the 30 to make another 50, double 50 is 100.

Very good again. Here's another:

3. $19 + 37 + 1 =$

> Hmm. This looks ever so hard but adding the 19 and 1 first makes it easy. 19 + 1 is 20 then another 37 makes 57.

Full marks, Zelda. And it all looks rather fun as well.

Something You May Have Noticed!
You can use lots of different words for adding.

> I noticed that notice, but only after I had banged my head on it.

These are some of them:

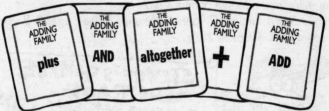

THE ADDING FAMILY **plus**   THE ADDING FAMILY **AND**   THE ADDING FAMILY **altogether**   THE ADDING FAMILY **+**   THE ADDING FAMILY **ADD**

All these can be put into an addition sum to mean the same thing. Here's the same sum written out in different ways to show you what we mean:

15 and 16 altogether makes 31

15 plus 16 equals 31

If I add 15 and 16 I get 31 altogether

15 + 16 = 31

Plus-fours

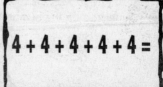

$4 + 4 + 4 + 4 + 4 =$

Plus Fours

MAKING ADDING AND SUBTRACTING EASIER

And as well as being lots of different way to say add – there are also lots of different ways to say subtract. Here are some of them:

All the subtraction words can be put into a subtraction sum to mean the same thing too. Here's exactly the same sum written out in different ways:

Subtract 3 from 5 leaves 2
Take away 3 from 5 and you end up with 2
3 is 2 less than 5
The difference between 5 and 3 is 2
Sam is 5 and Jamie is 3 so the difference in their ages is 2 years
5 count back 3 makes 2

The funny thing about subtraction – whichever word you use – is that you can use addition to work it out!

No we haven't lost our marbles. Look at this . . . for 24 – 17 you might say:

17 + 3 is 20 and add another 4 is 7, so the difference between 24 and 17 is 7.

Here's Superfrog on the number line to show you.

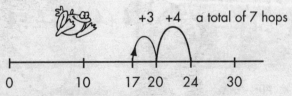

26

It works because addition is the reverse of subtraction. So as long as you check what you do, you can use any method of calculating you want! OK . . . now it's . . .

TUSSLE WITH THIS PUZZLE

Is this addition or subtraction?

Here's the puzzle. Colin has some ice-creams for Horace and Superfrog.

There are 9 ice-creams altogether. See them?

Now, he puts them all behind his back . . .

. . . and then just shows them 4 ice-creams.

How many can't they see behind his back?

He's hiding 5.

That's right Horace, he's hiding 5. But what did you do in your head to work that out? Can you remember?

Did you say:

9 take away 4 is 5.

9 minus something makes 4. Your teacher would probably write that like this: $9 - \square = 4$.

If I can see 4, I know that 4 and 5 is 9 so he must be hiding 5.

MAKING ADDING AND SUBTRACTING EASIER

Or did you do it a different way? The good news is – however you did it . . . that's OK!

Most calculations can be done in several different ways.

Hint 3 helps when you're working out what to do with missing bits of calculations.

Maths about missing bits is called algebra ∞. You can look up algebra in my glasses glossary at the back.

If $9 - \square = 4$ makes your knees wobble, don't worry. Learning how to do these sums with missing bits looks a lot harder than it is. It's easy to think this sign, =, means 'now write the answer'. But it doesn't mean that. It means 'balances' or 'equals', or 'is the same as'.

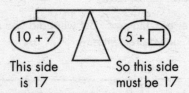

This side is 17   So this side must be 17

$$10 + 7 = 5 + \square$$

We call this a number sentence, or equation ∞.

Now, this equation reads '10 and 7 balance 5 and something'. We know both sides must balance, so if one side is $10 + 7 = 17$, then the other side must be made up to 17. At the moment there is just 5 on that side, so how can we find the missing number?

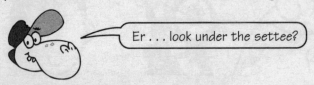

Er . . . look under the settee?

What do we need to add to 5 to make it up to 17?

$5 + \square = 17$

You can use this number line to help you.

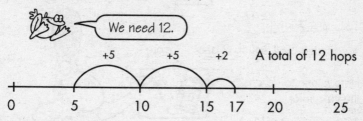

We need 12.

+5   +5   +2   A total of 12 hops

0   5   10   15 17 20   25

Well done, Superfrog.

Now look at these other balancing sums.

$6 + \square = 3 + 9$

Read the sentence carefully. 6 and something balance 3 and 9.
Have a go at it.

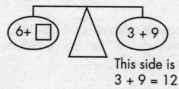

$6+\square$ $3 + 9$

This side is
$3 + 9 = 12$

You can do balancing sums
with any of the operations.
Remember, the four
operations are +, −, × and ÷.

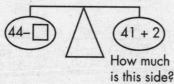

$44-\square$ $41 + 2$

How much
is this side?

$44 - \square = 41 + 2$

Read it carefully and have a go.

44 take away something balances 41 + 2. Take a peek at the
answers if your knees are wobbling. Then try the next one on your own.

$16 \div 4 = 2 + \square$

16 divided by 4 equals 2 and $\square$ more

Here is one to do on
the calculator.

$12 \times 12 = (10 \times 11) + \square$

> You need to work out the
> brackets first. That is one of
> the rules mathematicians have.

In a number sentence with different operations in it, mathematicians
will always do the brackets first, then any ÷, then any x, +, –.

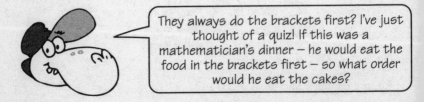

> They always do the brackets first? I've just
> thought of a quiz! If this was a
> mathematician's dinner – he would eat the
> food in the brackets first – so what order
> would he eat the cakes?

He would eat the eclairs first and then the buns and finally the slices of cake, assuming he wasn't on a diet of course.

Yes, very good Steven. That's an unusual way of looking at it, but it makes the point well. So, if we had the sum: 2 – (10 x 11) x 4 what order should you do it in?

You'd do the brackets first (10 x 11), then the multiplication by 4 and last the subtraction.

PUFFIN'S PECULIAR PUZZLE

Horace the Puffin has a puzzle.

Horace has 33 marbles and 2 bags exactly the same size.

He puts 15 of them in one bag and they fill the bag completely. He wants to get all the rest into the other bag which is exactly the same size. But it looks as though there are a lot of marbles left and he thinks they might not fit in. Will they all fit, or won't they?

An easy way to work this out is to ask 'what's double 15?' and see if there are any left over at the end.

Or you might say the total is 33. So it must be 15 add something makes 33, do you see? You could write it down like this: 15 + ☐ = 33. Remember that the = sign means 'balances'. So if we balance the sum – we find Horace has 18 left. So they won't all fit.

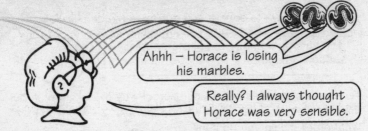

Ahhh – Horace is losing his marbles.

Really? I always thought Horace was very sensible.

Now for some good news. You don't actually have to do calculations the way your teacher taught you.

WHAT!!!

It's true. Look, perhaps you do sums like this at school:

20 –   and   999 –   and   1001 –
17   11   996

You might be taught things like 'do the units first', or get told about 'carrying' numbers.

Carry them where, mate?

Or you might find yourself doing this:

Cross out the nought, put a 9, now put a little 1 next to the 4 . . .

$$\begin{array}{r} 10\overset{9}{\cancel{0}}\overset{1}{4} \\ 996 \\ \hline \hline \end{array}$$

But you don't have to do this! You don't need to do calculations in a particular way, especially if you are doing them in your head.

Look, try these:

1.   1,004 – 996 =

See if you can do it in your head, or just with making little jottings in your notebook.

> **CLUE:**
> count up from
> 996, 997,
> 998, 999,
> 1000

Ah-ha – over here – a clue.

2.   9,999 – 3,333 =

> **CLUE:**
> picture this in your head.
> 9 units take away 3 units.
> Then do the same for the other columns.

Remember: the way you do calculations is up to you. You choose what you think will work best for each sum.

Exactly. Sometimes you need to learn quick ways to write things down so you can put them in your school maths book . . .

But!

. . . how you do it in your head is entirely up to you and you will probably be better at your ways than the ways someone teaches you.

MAKING ADDING AND SUBTRACTING EASIER

Now, what is rounding up and rounding down?

I know! Rounding up is when you eat too much pizza.

I've rounded myself up nicely thank you. No more pizza for me.

No, no it's not that, Steven. Rounding up or down means making numbers easier, often by making them into the nearest multiple of ten.

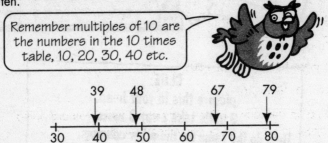

Remember multiples of 10 are the numbers in the 10 times table, 10, 20, 30, 40 etc.

Look at this number line. The nearest ten to 39 is 40. The nearest ten to 48 is 50 and the nearest to 87 is 90. So, what's the nearest ten to 99?

It's 100. See where it is on the next number line?

And rounding down is just like rounding up. If a number is closer to the ten below it than the ten above it, then you round down.

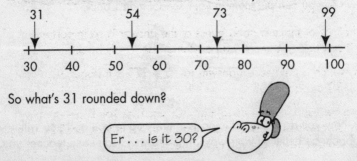

So what's 31 rounded down?

Er . . . is it 30?

Yes, well done. You've got the hang of it. What about rounding down 73?

70

Good. And what's 92 rounded down?

90. Hey this is easy! But hang on, what do you do if you have 35?

Good question. It depends a bit, but usually the fives are rounded up.

Rounding works with larger numbers too. You can round to the nearest 100 or even 1,000. The nearest 100 to 681 is 700. The nearest 1,000 to 3,212 is 3,000. Do you see? Have a go at these:

Round these to the nearest 10:

1. 77   2. 128   3. 459

Round these to the nearest 100:

4. 539   5. 989   6. 1,203

Rounding up and down is incredibly useful when you are doing calculations in your head or estimating something.

Always look at the number and ask yourself roughly how much the answer is going to be. You might find you don't need to write the sums down.

Estimating, or make a good guess at the answer is so important that it can help you more than anything else in this book!

Look, which is the nearest answer to 15 + 17? Is it about 20, about 30 or about 50?

It must be just a little bit more than 30, because you know double 15 is 30 and it is just a bit more than that. 32 in fact. See? By using what you already know you make it easier.

MAKING ADDING AND SUBTRACTING EASIER

OK, say you wanted to work out the sum: 601 + 1,001 = .
The first thing to do is to estimate. You could say, well, 601 is
about six hundred and 1,001 is about a thousand. 600 and 1,000
is going to be about 1,600 (one thousand six hundred).

So, now you know what the answer roughly is you won't make any
ridiculous mistakes that are miles out. In this sum, you can get to
the answer in your head, by seeing there are two more units to
add on. So the answer is 1,602 (one thousand, six hundred and
two). Do you see?

Let's try another one. Take the sum: 100 + 101 + 99 + 98 =
The first thing to do is to estimate. If you were going to add 100
and 101 and 99 and 98, you could round up the 99 and the 98
and say they are nearly a hundred. So the answer to this sum is
going to be somewhere about 400.

In fact the answer is 398.

Estimating is the same as asking yourself if you have reached a
sensible answer. So, if you were adding 15 and 17 and you got
the answer 18,000, you'd know you'd gone wrong somewhere!

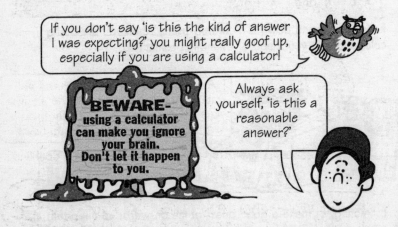

If you don't say 'is this the kind of answer
I was expecting?' you might really goof up,
especially if you are using a calculator!

BEWARE-
using a calculator
can make you ignore
your brain.
Don't let it happen
to you.

Always ask
yourself, 'is this a
reasonable
answer?'

Have a go at these. Estimate first.

1. 99 + 100 =
2. 79 + 80 =
3. 101 + 104 + 234 =
4. 1,001 – 999 =

If all these numbers are making your knees wobble, try thinking about money.

No, thinking about money like this, Steven. Say we have the sum 88 subtract 39. What would happen if you had £88 and you spent £39? How much would you have left? Some people find thinking about money makes it easier.

> Remember: the way you choose to do calculations will depend on the numbers and your favourite ways to calculate.

> We like doing near doubles so we'd add 15 and 16 by saying double 15 is 30 and then adding 1.

But what about the sum 238 + 9. Would you do that by doubling?

> No. We'd do 238 + 9 by adding 10 first then taking off the one.

OK. Now, choose how to do this sum yourself.

£88 – £39

How did you do it? There are several ways.

MAKING ADDING AND SUBTRACTING EASIER

1.

You could count back on a number line in your head until you get to 39.

49 hops altogether.

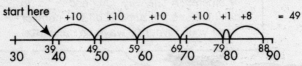

2.

You could do the opposite and count up on the number line, (and there is more than one way to do that counting up).

Thanks Superfrog, yes. And there are still several more ways you could do it.

3.

You could say 88 rounded up is 90 and 39 rounded up is 40. 90 take away 40 you know is 50, but now you must adjust from the rounding up.

Ohhh. That's the bit that gives me a headache. I don't know whether to take off the units I rounded up, or add them on.

Don't worry, Steven. Everyone has that problem. You'll get the hang on it. OK, Superfrog, what's another way you could do that sum?

4.

You could subtract the units first and say 88 take away 9 is easy because 88 – 10 is 78, but it was only subtract 9 not 10, so we have gone 1 too far, 79. Then take away the 30.

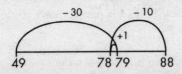

Or you could say, now I've got to 79, that is seven tens and nine units. I need to take the three tens from the 7 tens so that is 4 tens left, so that is 49 altogether.

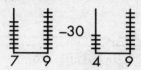

Or you could do it a completely different way. It's up to you!

MOT

Look at these calculations and decide which way you want to do them. They are a mixture of the things we have learnt so far. You might want to use:

REPAIR TOOLS

Doubling

Rounding Up and Rounding Down

Adding 10 first, to add 9 etc.

Remember to estimate first.

CLUE: the first one you can do by adding 10

1. 34 + 11 =

2. 67 + 9 =

3. 45 + 49 =

4. 259 + 301 =

5. 307 – 150 =

6. 569 + 70 =

7. 60 + 17 + 40 + 3 =

CLUE: pair up the numbers.

8. 149 + 58 + 150 + 2 =

9. 1,060 – 59 =

10. 226 + 75 =

MAKING ADDING AND SUBTRACTING EASIER

Always make calculations easier when you can.
Sometimes calculations are so complicated that you
need to write them down. Always make sure you
understand what you are writing.

Try to make sense of the sum in your head, and beware of methods
of writing down that you don't understand. You need to ask
someone if you get lost. Use blocks, pictures, or a number line to
help you if you wish.

Steven's trying to do 341 take away 176. He couldn't do it in his
head so he's using those hundreds tens and units blocks you see
at school.

Hundreds	Tens	Units
3	4	1

He exchanged a hundred block for ten tens and put those in the
tens column, then he exchanged one of those tens for units and
put those in the units column.

Hundreds	Tens	Units
2	13	11

So now he has 2 hundred blocks, 13 tens and 11 units. This is equal to the 342 that he started with. He hasn't taken away anything. He's just exchanged and moved things into different columns.

200 + 130 (13 tens) and 11 units is equal to 341.

Now he's got the blocks in different columns, he can take away the 176.

> Shall we estimate first? 341 is almost 350, take away a bit less than 200, so the answer needs to be about 150.

OK, Steven, now have a go at taking away the 176.

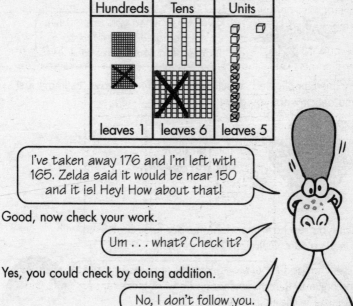

Hundreds	Tens	Units
leaves 1	leaves 6	leaves 5

> I've taken away 176 and I'm left with 165. Zelda said it would be near 150 and it is! Hey! How about that!

Good, now check your work.

> Um . . . what? Check it?

Yes, you could check by doing addition.

> No, I don't follow you.

Well, start with your answer of 165, then add back the 176 and see what happens.

$$165 +$$
$$\underline{176}$$
$$\underline{341}$$

> Hey! I got back to 341.

Very good. Now, can you see another way to do that calculation?

MAKING ADDING AND SUBTRACTING EASIER

What about a number line?

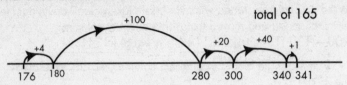

total of 165

You could count up from 176. First, add 4. Then jump in easy 10s until you get to 340. Then another 1. Adding up all those jumps comes to 165.

Your estimate and our check showed us you're right – the answer is 165.

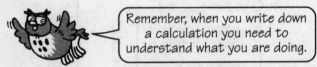

Remember, when you write down a calculation you need to understand what you are doing.

Try this complicated calculation two different ways. Estimate first and check what you do.

672 – 383 =

Hint 5

You can do it any way you like.

Can you see how important number lines are? Even with complicated calculations they can help.

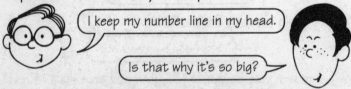

I keep my number line in my head.

Is that why it's so big?

Number lines can go below zero. They are a bit like a thermometer that can show very cold temperatures. Numbers below zero are called negative numbers.

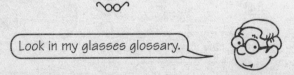

Look in my glasses glossary.

Look at this thermometer. What was the temperature for the night and the day?

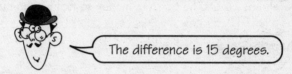

At night it was minus five degrees and in the day it was ten degrees.

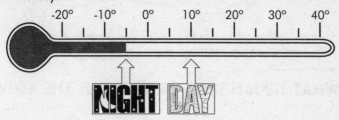

The difference is 15 degrees.

Numbers can go below zero with money too. Here's a story. Colin's mum looks after his bank box. Sometimes she lends him money. Colin has £27. He wants to buy a new computer programme. Here it is:

He only has £27 so his mum lends him £3. But now he's broken a window and has to pay his mum another £17. Can you work out how much he owes his Mum altogether?
(There's a number line over the page which will help!)

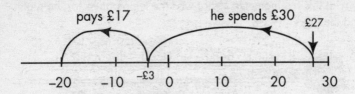

WHAT DOUGH DOES HE OWE FOR THE YO-YO?

Try these.

1. Colin has £10, he spends £24. By how much is he in debt?
2. Steven has £6 and he borrows money so that he can buy a new yo-yo for £10. By how much is he in debt?

OK, now, look at this number line:

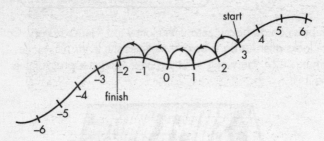

3. If you count back 5 from 3 where do you end up?
4. If you count on from minus 6, three steps forward, where do you end up?
5. If you start on 1 and hop back 4 steps where do you land?

You can use any numbers you want on a number line.

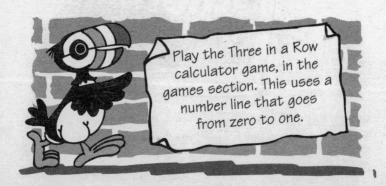

Play the Three in a Row calculator game, in the games section. This uses a number line that goes from zero to one.

44

COLIN'S CHALKBOARD CONCLUSIONS

1. You don't have to do calculations the way your teacher taught you!

2. Always look at the number and ask yourself roughly how much the answer is going to be. You might find you don't need to write the sums down.

3. The way you choose to do calculations will depend on the numbers and your favourite ways to calculate.

4. Sometimes calculations are so complicated that you need to write them down. Make sure you understand what you are writing.

Colin I've estimated something. Will you help me see if I'm right?

Yes.

Estimate 8/10 hits

Good. Just shut your eyes and don't open them until I say.

Getting a Grip on
Multiplying and Dividing

I can't do tables tests. I always get stuck. My legs turn to jelly and when my teacher asks me questions my mind goes blank.

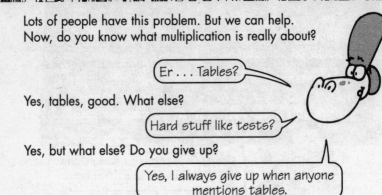

Lots of people have this problem. But we can help. Now, do you know what multiplication is really about?

Er . . . Tables?

Yes, tables, good. What else?

Hard stuff like tests?

Yes, but what else? Do you give up?

Yes, I always give up when anyone mentions tables.

Well, look at this then. Multiplication means multiple-addition and is all about 'lots of'. So, 5 lots of 4 means; 4 and another 4 and another 4 and another 4 and another 4. You could write this 4 + 4 + 4 + 4 + 4 (5 lots of 4).

But if we did all multiplications like that and we had to write down something like 37 lots of 9 this way you would get tired and your maths book would be filled up in a week.

Just bringing back last night's homework.

CLASS 6M MATHS BOOKS

Now, you can see it's much quicker not to do a long sum of adding but to write 5 x 4 or 4 x 5. It doesn't matter whether you see it as 4 lots of 5 or 5 lots of 4.

The pictures are very different, but the answer is the same.

This is 4 lots of 5 footballs. 20 footballs altogether.

This is 5 lots of 4 footballs. 20 footballs altogether.

See if you can write these a quicker way:

1. 2 + 2 + 2 + 2 + 2 + 2 + 2
2. 3 + 3 + 3 + 3 + 3 + 3 + 3 + 3 + 3 + 3 + 3

OK, that was quite easy. Is there anything else about multiplication that is easy?

Yes, yes, yes, yes . . . Yes. Oh yes. Yes.

Multiplying by 10, 100 and 1000 is really easy. Look:

3 x 10 is 30   You just add a zero to the number.
3 x 100 is 300   You just add 2 zeros to the number.
3 x 1,000 is 3,000 Guess what? You add 3 zeros.

I expect you can work out what to do to multiply a number by ten thousand.

3. 3 x 10,000 =

And what about by a hundred thousand?

4. 8 x 100,000 =

Try some more. Count the zeros carefully!

5. 7 x 10 =
6. 5 x 10 =
7. 14 x 100 =
8. 78 x 1,000 =

MULTIPLYING AND DIVIDING

OK. So multiplication means 'lots of' and numbers with zeros in them are easy.

> Yeah – that helps but how can I be expected to remember all those numbers in the tables?

Good question. Here are some **TEACHERS' SECRETS** that should definitely help.

> Look – I've remembered all my tables.

TEACHERS' SECRETS 1

Guess what? There is a link between multiplying and dividing just like there is a link between adding and subtracting.

Multiplication undoes division. So, 7 x 8 is 56 and 56 ÷ 8 is 7.

Here's another one. 9 x 7 is 63, so we know that 63 ÷ 7 is 9 and 63 ÷ 9 is 7.

Dividing is tables backwards!

More about this in Colin's Magic 3 Number Game on page 58.

TEACHERS' SECRETS 2

Multiplication and division are opposites so they can be used for checking each other. Checking is very important.

> I've just checked Colin.

Yes, not those sort of checks, Steven. Checking to make sure you have the right answer. So if you divide 24 by 6 and you get the answer 4, you can check if you are right by remembering your tables, 4 x 6 is 24.

And if you're wondering how this will help you do your tables tests better, here's the third 'Teachers' Secret'. . .

 **TEACHERS' SECRETS 3**

Think about the tables that link together. So some numbers in the 2 x table are in the 4 x table and also the 6 x, the 8 x and the 10 x table.

1	**2**	3	**④**	5	**6**	7	**⑧**	9	**10**
11	**⑫**	13	**14**	15	**⑯**	17	**18**	19	**⑳**
21	**22**	23	**㉔**	25	**26**	27	**㉘**	29	**30**

KEY

Numbers in bold are in the 2 x table

Numbers with a ◯ around them are in the 4 x table

It'll be really clear if you do this: make a hundred square and use coloured pens to show the different tables. You could colour all the 2 x table in yellow. Then circle the 4 x numbers blue and the 8 x numbers green. Some squares will be multi-coloured!

Look at 24. It's a very special number. Which tables is 24 in?*

Now look at how the 5 x and the 10 x are linked.

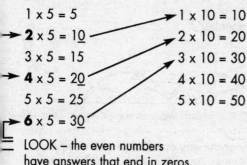

1 x 5 = 5

2 x 5 = 1<u>0</u>

3 x 5 = 15

4 x 5 = 2<u>0</u>

5 x 5 = 25

6 x 5 = 3<u>0</u>

1 x 10 = 10

2 x 10 = 20

3 x 10 = 30

4 x 10 = 40

5 x 10 = 50

6 lots of 5 is 30.
30 is 3 lots of 10.

LOOK – the even numbers have answers that end in zeros.

DETECT WHICH CONNECT!

Which other tables are linked?

1. Which ones are linked to the 3 x table?
2. Which ones are linked to the 4 x table?

Try to remember about these links. It is very useful and means you don't have to learn lots of facts.

*Answer: 2, 3, 4, 6, and 8 (and 12 and 24) times tables.

MULTIPLYING AND DIVIDING

Right – come on Steven – what is 6 lots of 7?

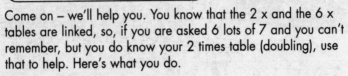

Aaugghh! I think I've some flower arranging to do.

Come on – we'll help you. You know that the 2 x and the 6 x tables are linked, so, if you are asked 6 lots of 7 and you can't remember, but you do know your 2 times table (doubling), use that to help. Here's what you do.

Double 7 is 14 (doubling is the 2 x table), so that is 2 lots of 7. We need 6 lots of 7 altogether. So that is three lots of double 7.

1 lot of double 7 is 14
2 lots of double 7 is 14 + 14 = 28
3 lots of double 7 is 28 + 14 = 42

6 lots of 7

o o o o o o o   double 7
o o o o o o o   is 14

o o o o o o o   2 lots of double
o o o o o o o   7 is 28

o o o o o o o   3 lots of double 7
o o o o o o o   is 42

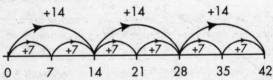

Let's look at another one. Suppose you don't know your 6 times table, but you know your 3 times. You can't work out 9 times 6, but you know that 9 x 3 is 27. Well, 9 times 6 would be double that. Double 27 is 54.

111	9 x 3 = 27
111	27 doubled is 54
111	
111	
111	
111	
111	
111	
111	

Make sure you learn your doubles up to 100.

Tables – your time starts now.

Right, there are other ways you can make calculations easier too. Look at this. To multiply by 25 you could multiply by 100 then halve and halve again.

Look, 25 times 16 looks hard, but you can do it like this. It is really easy to multiply by 100 (look back to page 47 if you have forgotten). So 16 times 100 is 1600. Halving that makes 800. Half that again is 400.

It works because 25 is half of a half of 100. Here's another one.

23 times 20 looks hard, but you can split the 23 into 20 and 3.
20 times 20 is easy and makes 400
3 times 20 is 60
so the answer is 460.

So the thing to do is to think about what you already know, and what is easy to do and work out harder sums from that.

But what can I do if my mind goes blank in a tables test?

Well, there are several things you can do. You can:

1. Work it out as 'lots of'. So 16 x 3 is 16 lots of 3.

111 111 111 111
111 111 111 111
111 111 111 111
111 111 111 111   16 lots of 3

Draw them out like this if you want.

MULTIPLYING AND DIVIDING

2. Think of an easier way to do the calculation such as splitting up the number.

3. And you can always check by doing division.

> Division is the opposite of multiplication.

There are just a few more important things.

> Oh no, I've got brain overload.

But some of this is easy! Look!

1. Any number multiplied by zero is zero.

    Twelve million, eight hundred and sixty-three thousand and forty-eight multiplied by zero is zero.

2. Remember we said that x and ÷ are linked? Well, you can't divide by zero. You just can't do it. Asking what 345 divided by zero is, is like asking someone to tell you the largest number ever. You just can't do it.

3. There is one thing that is very different about x and ÷. You can multiply in any order. 2 x 6 is the same as 6 x 2 . . .

> But!

. . . this doesn't work with division.

32 ÷ 2 is 16

If you had 32 sweets and divided them between 2 people they'd have 16 each.

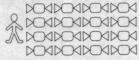 

But 2 ÷ 32 is very different.

If you had 2 sweets and divided them between 32 people they'd have . . . well only a couple of licks each. Yugghh!

4.   The other slightly tricky thing is that division has two different meanings.

Oh no!

But it's not that hard. Division can be sharing or grouping. It's like this:

i) Sharing

Sharing is like the sweets we were sharing. 32 divided between 2 people can mean 32 shared between 2 so you get 16 each. This is about fair sharing so that everyone gets the same amount.

ii) Grouping

Grouping is a bit different and you say it a bit differently. 32 ÷ 2 can mean: 'If I have 32 sweets, to how many people can I give 2 each'. You see, the numbers are the same, but the meaning is different.

If there were 18 people, tough on the last two! I've only got enough for 16 people. This is because it was decided that the size of the 'group' was 2. So this 'grouping' aspect of sharing is less about 'equal sharing' and more about sizes of group being decided before the start.

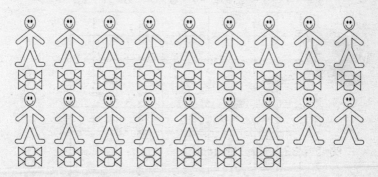

Don't worry too much about this if it sends you brain into overload. Just know there are two meanings when you see the division sign and listen for which one is in the sum you are working out – the question will make it clear.

MULTIPLYING AND DIVIDING

Remember that there are rather a lot of different signs and words for division. Here are some of them:

Here's the same sum written out different ways:

60 ÷ 10 or

10 ⌐ 60   (how many tens in 60?)

or 60
   ――
   10

Now . . . Impress your friends with . . .

Super fast multiplication. No sweat. This is an empty multiplication square. Don't fill it in!

X	1	2	3	4	5	6	7	8	9	10
1										
2										
3										
4										
5										
6										
7										
8										
9										
10										

Stage 1

Ask for some squared paper (you can use lined paper and a ruler) and copy the empty multiplication square. It will help if you can get someone to photocopy you about twenty copies of it. (Most adults are so hung up about you learning your tables that they will probably make you two hundred copies.)

I think that's enough now thanks.

Make a time chart like this one.

ZELDA'S TIME CHART

Time taken	minutes	seconds
Day 1	18	22
Day 2	17	59
Day 3		

Stage 2

Take one multiplication square and start to fill it in just like this one.

X	1	2	3	**4**	5
1	1	2	3	4	5
2	2	4	6	8	10
3	3	6	9	**12**	
4					

You work out the number to put in the square by looking at the top number and the side number.
4 x 3 = 12

Time yourself and write the time down.

Then do it again with another blank square and try to be faster. Keep doing it until you are so fast that you are only knocking off fractions of a second each time you do it.

MULTIPLYING AND DIVIDING

Stage 3

Keep the top line of numbers the same (2, 3, 4 and so on) but
change the side numbers so that the tables are all muddled up.

X	1	2	3	4	5	6	7	8	9	10
5										
7										
11										
2										

Keep practising that until you are faster than anyone else in your family.

Stage 4
Advanced game for those who want to be much faster at tables than any of their teachers and show them up.

Muddle up both the
top and the
side numbers.

X	2	8	10	9
6				
9				
4				

You'll also need to learn all the
multiplication and division words if you
are going to do brilliantly in tests.

Here are all the words you need to know. Write them down and stick
them on your mirror and learn them every day for a week.

THE DIVISION FAMILY **divide**
THE DIVISION FAMILY **share equally**
THE DIVISION FAMILY **factor**
THE DIVISION FAMILY **÷**
THE MULTIPLICATION FAMILY **times**
THE MULTIPLICATION FAMILY **product**
THE MULTIPLICATION FAMILY **multiple**
THE MULTIPLICATION FAMILY **X**
THE MULTIPLICATION FAMILY **lots of**

The factors ∽∞∾ of a number are all the numbers that divide into it exactly, without leaving a remainder eg 3 x 5 = 15
3 and 5 are both factors of 15.

A product ∽∞∾ is the number when two or more numbers are multiplied together.
2 x 3 = 6   6 is the product.

MOT

Get an adult to read these questions to you. Time yourself as you write down the answers. Then ask them to read it to you again next week and see if you can get quicker.

Then do it again but ask them to change the numbers. Time yourself, then try to do it faster.

1. Double 33.
2. Double 56.
3. Double 79.
4. Half of 36.
5. Half of 34.
6. Half of 32.
7. 25 times 4 is 100 so what is 100 divided by 4?
8. 56 divided into 8 groups is 7 in a group so what is 7 x 8?
9. Write the next 4 multiples of 6 after 12.
10. Which number has factors 1, 2, 3, 4, 6 and 12 and no other?
11. What is the product of 3 and 7?
12. Share 48 equally between 4.
13. Divide 42 by 7.
14. 16 lots of 3.
15. 9 times 4.
16. 10 multiplied by 100.
17. How many bits of ribbon 50 cm long can I cut from 3 metres 10 cm? How much is left over?
18. What is the product of 7 and 11?
19. Which number multiplied by 3 gives 27?
20. A number multiplied by itself is 64. What is the number?
21. When I divide my number by 5, I get 6 groups and 1 left over. What is my number?

22. The product of two numbers is 24. What could the numbers be? There are several answers.
23. How many 4s in 36?
24. Divide 366 by 6.
25. Does 5 go into 226 with none left over?
26. Monster has 60 sweets. To how many people can he give 2?
27. <u>15</u> (please read this as 15 over 3)
    3
28. $7\overline{)42}$

    (please read this as how many times does 7 go into 42?)
29. Write four different calculations using x and ÷ and just the numbers 7, 9 and 63.
30. Is 63 a multiple of 9?

When you know all these words for multiplication and division, you will really impress your friends.

HOW TO PLAY COLIN'S MAGIC 3 NUMBER GAME

Think of a multiplication sum.

How about 9 x 2 is 18?

OK. You can only use those three numbers, 2, 9 and 18 and you have to write four different sums, just using those numbers.

Do it in four columns like this. Or ask someone to listen to your answers.

9 x 2 = 18   2 x 9 = 18   18 ÷ 2 = 9   18 ÷ 9 = 2

Do you get it? Try these. You can use the 4 columns.

1. 3, 4, 12
2. 6, 7, 42
3. 3, 9, 27

Doing maths in your head is often quicker than writing. Have you noticed that almost all of the calculations in this section you have been able to work out in your head? Doing the working out on paper for things like this . . .

$$\begin{array}{r} 16 \\ \times\ \ 2 \\ \hline 2 \\ {\scriptstyle 1} \end{array}$$

2 x 6 is 12 so I put down the 2 and carry a little 1 and put this under the line . . .

Well, it's just silly. You can do this in your head! No-one needs to carry ones anywhere. Anyway, it's a ten that you put in the tens column.

But!

Some calculations you will need to write down, even if it is just to keep adults happy. However, try to persuade them that you can write it down any way you want at first and you will get faster at it as time goes by.

I must do an estimate first. Suppose the sum is 18 x 3. Now – roughly what answer am I expecting from 18 x 3?

Well – 18 x 3 is a bit less than 20 x 3 and that is 60 because 20 x 3 is 60. Now – I'm going to split up the 18 into 10 and 8
10 x 3 = 30   8 x 3 = 24

I add them together 30 + 24 is 54. Yes, that looks right. A bit less than 60. Now let's check. How many 3s in 54?
54 ÷ 3 = 18.

Hey I'm right!

At some schools they make you write down calculations in just one way. Adults are a bit funny like that, but do it anyway. If you don't understand what they did, yell.

ADVANCED MOT

More amazing doubling!

1. Doubling 15

I'm doubling this number.   So double this number.

$\underline{1}$ x 15 =   15 so
$\underline{2}$ x 15 =   30 so
$\underline{4}$ x 15 =   60 so
$\underline{8}$ x 15 =   120

How far can you go?

2. Now try the same thing with 25

1 x 25 = 25 so
2 x 25 = 50 so
4 x 25 = 100 so
8 x 25 and so on. Go on as far as you can.

256 x 25 would be a good place to get to.

3. What is the number you need to multiply 25 by to get to a million ∞?

Even when it looks hard, you can probably make it easier.

Here is another clever way to work out tables facts for larger tables. Take a table you don't often have to learn at school, like 12. (Most adults had to learn their 12 times at school and they get a bit hot under the collar about it so you need to keep them happy.)

Show them this bit of amazing maths.

To work out the 12 times table you can add the answers in the 2 times to the answers in the 10 times like this.

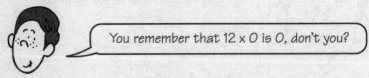

You remember that 12 x 0 is 0, don't you?

1 x 12 is 12	1 x 2 is 2 and 1 x 10 is 10	2 + 10 = 12
2 x 12 is 24	2 x 2 is 4 and 2 x 10 is 20	4 + 20 = 24
3 x 12 is 36	3 x 2 is 6 and 3 x 10 is 30	6 + 30 = 36

and so on.

Try these.

1. 4 x 12 =
2. 5 x 12 =
3. See if you can get to 12 x 12.

Of course, this works with any number. You could work out the 17 times table by adding the 7 times answers to the 10 times answers.

Multiplying by 9 and 11

Remember how you learnt to add 9 and 11 by adding 10 first and then adding or taking one away? (It's on page 11.)

Well, you can do very clever multiplying by 9 and 11 in a similar way. Look at this.

14 x 11 can look a bit hard. But you can multiply it by 10 like this: 14 x 10 is 140 (so that is 10 lots of 14). You need another lot of 14 to make 11 lots of 14 so add another 14.

140 + 14 = 154. That is the answer to 14 x11. Clever eh?

To multiply by 9, do times 10 first and then take off whatever your number is.

Look, 17 x 9 can be done by saying, 17 times 10 is 170, but that is 10 lots of 17 and I only wanted 9 lots of 17 so I need to take one lot of 17 away.

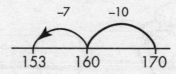

170 take off 10 is 160 take off another 7 is 153.

ONLY FOR STUDENTS WHOSE KNEES ARE NOT WOBBLING

Multiplying by 21 and 19

You'll look unbelievably clever if you can do something like multiply by 21 and 19. You multiply by 20 and then adjust by taking away or adding. If your brain is groaning, ignore this, but here is one way to multiply 13 by 21.

13 x 21 = 13 x 20 and then one more lot of 13

= 260 + 13

= 273.

And if you really want to show off

That's me!

Instead of multiplying some large difficult numbers – you use really easy numbers that are close to them. Here's what we mean:

49 and 51 are both close to 50. So you could work out 8 x 49 by multiplying by 50 first.

8 lots of 50 is easy, because it's the same as 4 lots of 100, which is 400. Then take off the extra 8. 400 – 8 = 392.

So for 99 and 101 you could multiply by 100.

Exactly. 37 x 101 is 37 x 100 add another 37= 3,737.

COLIN'S CHALKBOARD CONCLUSIONS

1. Multiplication is about 'lots of'.

2. Learning tables is easier when you think of all the numbers that are related to each other.

3. If you know your tables you can also do division because division is the opposite of multiplication.

4. Always try to make calculations easier.

5. You can do multiplications in any order, but not divisions.

Hey Colin — what's double two?

Four!

No. Tu-tu!

Messing About with
Numbers

Number patterns

Lots of maths is about finding patterns. Some patterns are quite easy to spot. Look at this one.

1st   **2nd**   **3rd**

As you can see, there are 5 footballs in the 3rd pattern.

Hint: Do you remember the pattern of odd numbers? (see page 13)

ODD BALLS

1. How many balls would you need to make the 4th pattern?
2. How many did you add to the 3rd pattern to make the 4th?
3. How many in the 5th pattern?
4. What about the 20th pattern?
5. And the 100th?

Tell someone how you know those answers.

Did you know you already know lots of other number patterns? Look at this one. 2, 4, 6, 8. You know what comes next. It's 10, 12, 14.

All the numbers that can be shared evenly between 2 people are even numbers. They end in 2, 4, 6, 8, 0. All other numbers are odd.

Some patterns are a bit harder and some are very hard. In this section you will find out about perfect numbers and prime numbers and some mathematicians spend most of their life trying to work out the next numbers in those patterns!

Function machines

Now, do you know what a function machine is?

> Is it a sort of machine that goes to functions and chats politely when the Mayor is tired and doesn't want to bother?

It's something mathematicians sometimes talk about when they get onto the subject of number sequences. An easy way to imagine these function machines is to think of them as robots which obey instructions we give them. For example – meet this function machine called Mac. Colin's giving Mac something to do.

> Obey me and multiply all numbers that go in by 9.

1. Which numbers will come out when 4, 5, 6 and 7 go in?

2. If you keep going with the x 9 pattern, do you think you will land on 200?

3. Look at the special pattern we get with answers to the 9 x table.

MESSING ABOUT WITH NUMBERS

Start with the answers to the 9 x table.

9	0 add 9 is 9
1 8	add the 1 and 8 = 9
2 7	add the 2 + 7 = 9
3 6	add the 3 + 6 = 9

Go on with this adding pattern and then check your answers in the back.

Now let's get back to Mac, the function machine. Zelda's giving Mac another task.

> Double numbers and add one!

4. Which numbers will come out next? These numbers have a special name. Can you remember it?

> Does the machine do anything you tell it to? Machine — make me a chocolate cake!

Puzzles, and Problems

Playing around with numbers can help you get very good at maths in your head. Here is quite an easy puzzle to kick off.

Can you draw a line right across this watch face so that the numbers on each side of the line add up to the same number?

Horace the Puffin had a go — but got it wrong. Bad luck Horace.

AMAZE PEOPLE WITH THESE 'THINK OF A NUMBER' PUZZLES.

1. Think of any number (say 5) and then do this to it:
    subtract 2 $5 - 2 = 3$
    multiply the new number by 3 $3 \times 3 = 9$
    add 12 $9 + 12 = 21$
    divide that number by 3
    (OK, get a calculator to check if you
    really need to . . . but you DON'T   3 into 21 = 7
    need a calculator for this one.)
    add 5 (without a calculator!) $7 + 5 = 12$
    then subtract the number you first thought of
    (we did 5 in this example). $12 - 5 = 7$
    Our finishing number is 7.

Now try several times with other numbers.

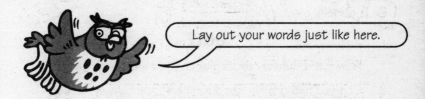

Lay out your words just like here.

Puzzled? Get a grown up interested and see if they can explain it.
Don't worry if you or they can't understand it! It's a trick!

AMAZE YOUR FRIENDS WHO DON'T OFTEN GET AMAZED!

Here is another one. Take any five consecutive numbers (e.g. 1,2,3,4,5)
and find the total.
Divide the number by 5.
Subtract 2.
What happens?

Try it with different numbers, e.g. $3 + 4 + 5 + 6 + 7$.
Then try $4 + 5 + 6 + 7 + 8$.

MESSING ABOUT WITH NUMBERS

Making rectangles

Some numbers are good for making rectangles. With 12 squares you can make 3 different rectangles.

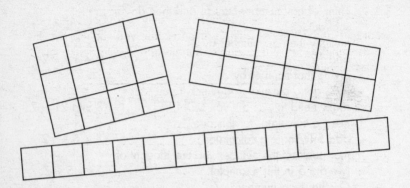

Some numbers are hopeless for making rectangles except for a rectangle just with one row. Try 11 squares. Hopeless.

24 is a really great number.

QUIZ

1. How many different rectangles can you make with 24?

2. Can you find another good number?

3. Can you find a number that makes 5 rectangles?

OK, now which numbers are good for making rectangles, those in times tables or those not in times tables?

Over here, Watson!

CLUE:
is 19 in any
times tables
you learn?

The numbers in multiplication tables are the best ones for making rectangles. But any number will make a rectangle of just one line. These numbers that *only* make one line are called prime numbers. Look at these.

5 and 7 are prime numbers because they only make one line, so are 11 and 13. But 9 isn't a prime because you can make a 3 by 3 rectangle. Yes, it is a square, but any shape with right angles is called a rectangle.

Mathematicians don't call 1 a prime number, but 2 is – 2 is the only even prime number.

4. Go on with this list of prime numbers.
   2, 3, 5, 7, 11, 13.

CHALLENGE.
THIS IS A REALLY TOUGH ONE.

5. Is 519 a prime number?

Yes, thanks, Steven. You can use your calculator here.

Perfect numbers

How can a number be perfect?

Good question. Now, remember about factors ∿∞∾? You multiply factors when you do times tables. So the factors of 6 are 1, 2, 3 and 6. That's because 1 x 6 is 6 and 2 x 3 is 6. See?

Here's another example. The factors of 12 are 1, 2, 3, 4, 6 and 12.

6 is a perfect number because if you add up the factors except for 6, you get 6.

1+ 2 + 3 = 6

12 isn't a perfect number because if you add up the factors of 12 (but not 12 itself) you don't get 12, you get 16. Like this:
1 + 2 + 3 + 4 + 6 = 16. So 12 is not a perfect number.

BASIC MOT

1. The next perfect number after 6 is less than 40. Try to find it.
2. Now, if we were really mean we could ask you to find the next perfect number, but we aren't that mean. But just in case you want to try, the next two perfect numbers are in the answers.

FIZZ IN THIS QUIZ

Find a pair of numbers with:
1. a sum of 14 and a product of 49.

That's the same as saying: 'Two numbers that when you add them together make 14, and when you multiply them together make 49.'

2. a sum of 16 and a product of 60.
3. a sum of 22 and a product of 57.

Find a pair of numbers with:

4. a difference of 12 and a product of 45.
5. a difference of 0 and a product of 144.
6. a difference of 22 and a product of 75.

Be great when you estimate

We're not going to let you forget how important estimating is.
You can make guesses about operations (+, −, x and ÷). Work
out the right sign for these numbers. Make a guess first. Look
carefully at the numbers, and look for a reasonable answer.

And no using a calculator.

1.	321	☐	289	=	610
2.	54	☐	156	=	8424
3.	507	☐	13	=	39
4.	895	☐	56	=	839

FRUSTRATING CHALLENGE

If you were only allowed to use the numbers 1, 2, 3, 4 (in any
order) could you make all the numbers from 0 to 20? Here are all
the rules.

RULES

**You can put the numbers in any order.
You must use all of the numbers for each calculation.
You are only allowed to use each number once.
You can use any operation or mix of operations
(+ − x or ÷)**

So, under those rules, the number 8 could be made like this:

4 + 3 + 2 − 1 = 8

And you can also use negative numbers. So, 4 – 3 is 1 take away 2 gets you to minus 1 then add 1 makes 0. You can write that as 4 – 3 – 2 + 1 = 0.

It looks like this on the number line:

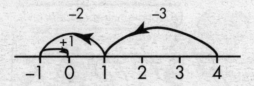

Sometimes you will need brackets as well. Remember brackets are always done first (see page 30). So, to make 16 you can do (4 x 2) makes 8, then (3 – 1) makes 2 so 8 x 2 = 16.

We write this as (4 x 2) x (3 – 1) = 16

Now, go for it: make all the numbers from 0 to 20!

REALLY FRUSTRATING CHALLENGE

This second frustrating challenge is similar but the rules are much stricter! Take all the digits from 1 to 9 and try to make 100. These are the rules:

RULES

You must use the digits in the order 1 2 3 4 5 6 7 8 9.
You must use all the digits.
You can put digits together to make other numbers.
So, 1 and 2 could go together to make 12, or 5, 6 and 7 could make 567.
You must only use + or –.
You can only use each digit once.

Happy thinking!!!!

COLIN'S CHALKBOARD CONCLUSIONS

The more you play around with numbers, the better you will get at maths. You will find that if you try to make a good guess first, you are more likely to get your answers right.

If someone shouts four followed by another four, have you got eight?

No — you've got Colin playing golf. Take cover!

Fore!

Help! I Can't Do Fractions!!

Fractions can look really hard.

> Fractions? Yughghgh!

Yes, it can definitely make your knees wobble when people start talking about quarters, thirds, eighths or fifths. So we're going to show you what they're all about and why they're not so bad after all.

So what actually is a fraction?

> Something nasty.

All right, Steven, here's a question: would you rather have one quarter or one eighth of a chocolate cake?

> Chocolate cake. Hmm!

Before you can answer that question you need to know how big each bit is. These pictures should help you.

A cake which is cut into 4 equal pieces is divided into quarters (or fourths). One of those pieces is called one quarter. We write that as $\frac{1}{4}$.

A cake which is cut into 8 equal pieces is divided into eighths. One of those pieces is called one eighth. We write that as $\frac{1}{8}$.

A cake cut into 10 equal pieces is divided into tenths. One of these pieces is called a tenth. We write that as $\frac{1}{10}$.

Tenths are very important for decimals, and also for working with computers and calculators.

> If I cut the cake into a hundred pieces would each bit be called a hundredth?

Exactly, Colin. Now concentrate. Is a hundredth of the cake smaller or larger than a quarter?

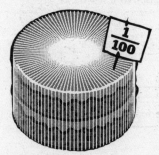 

The answer is it's smaller – a quarter is much bigger.

Now, the number on the bottom of the fraction is called the denominator. This number tells you how many pieces the cake is cut into. The number on the top (the numerator) tells you how many pieces you are going to get (if you're lucky!!).

    1   this is the numerator

    —

    3   this is the denominator

So, if you have $\frac{1}{3}$ of a cake you have one piece when the cake has been cut into 3 equal pieces.

FRACTIONS

USE YOUR WITS TO SPOT THE BITS

How many pieces would a cake be cut into if it was in:

1. thirds $\frac{1}{3}$
2. fifths $\frac{1}{5}$
3. tenths $\frac{1}{10}$

 You will need to remember tenths for later, for the decimals chapter!!

4. nineteenths $\frac{1}{19}$
5. thirteenths $\frac{1}{13}$
6. thirtieths $\frac{1}{30}$

Now, which is bigger?

You can draw pictures to help you if you need them.

7. $\frac{1}{3}$ or $\frac{1}{5}$ 8. $\frac{1}{3}$ or $\frac{1}{2}$ 9. $\frac{1}{6}$ or $\frac{1}{7}$

10. $\frac{1}{4}$ or $\frac{1}{2}$ 11. $\frac{1}{9}$ or $\frac{1}{3}$ 12. $\frac{1}{3}$ or $\frac{1}{8}$

Did you notice anything about those fractions? Well, look at them again but this time, look at where they come on a number line.

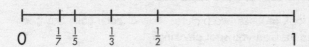

Draw the number line in your notebook and then put on other numbers, such as $\frac{1}{9}$ and $\frac{1}{10}$. You can take a peek at the answers if you get stuck.

I expect you can see that the bigger the denominator (the number on the bottom) the smaller the fraction (or the piece of cake) and the nearer that fraction is to zero.

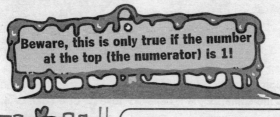

Beware, this is only true if the number at the top (the numerator) is 1!

Yes, if the numerator is 1, then the bigger the denominator, the smaller the fraction.

Lost? Well, if you have $\frac{2}{3}$ of a cake, how much do you have?

The cake is still split into 3 equal pieces but this time you have 2 pieces instead of one. The numerator tells you this. $\frac{2}{3}$. See?

Yeah I see. Mmm, yummy!

FRACTIONS

Fractions that are the same size

Now, look at these two pictures. Part of each cake has been shaded in. Can you spot anything?

Hmm – let's see . . .

Even though they are split into different size pieces the bit that is shaded is the same. So, is it better to have $\frac{1}{2}$ of a cake or $\frac{2}{4}$ of a cake?

It doesn't matter because they are the same size.

Exactly, Colin.

So how can you find pairs that are the same? You just divide the top and bottom by the same number.

Look – like this:

$$\frac{3 \div 3}{9 \div 3} \qquad \frac{1}{3}$$

so $\frac{3}{9}$ is the same as $\frac{1}{3}$

Would you rather have $\frac{2}{3}$ of a cake or $\frac{4}{6}$?

They are the same size!

THE GAME'S TO FIND THE SAME

$$\frac{1}{3} \quad \frac{1}{2} \quad \frac{2}{8} \quad \frac{4}{8}$$

$$\frac{1}{4} \quad \frac{1}{2} \quad \frac{3}{6} \quad \frac{2}{6}$$

Pick a fraction from the number cloud to make each answer.

1.   .... is the same size as $\frac{1}{3}$

2.   .... is the same size as $\frac{1}{2}$

3.   .... is the same size as $\frac{4}{8}$

4.   .... is the same size as $\frac{2}{8}$

Peek at the answers if your knees are wobbling. Next week do it on your own.

Finding a fraction of a number

Sometimes you will be asked to find fractions of a number of things like $\frac{1}{2}$ of 8. This is really easy! How would you find a half of a bag of footballs? You just split them into 2 equal groups like this.

So, $\frac{1}{2}$ of 8 is 4 because there are 4 things in each group. See? Another way to think of this is dividing 8 into 2 groups or $8 \div 2 = 4$.

Now, what about other fractions? To find $\frac{1}{3}$ (a third) of a group of 12 penguins, divide all the penguins into 3 equal groups like this.

I'm c-c-c-c-c-c-c-cold.

There are 4 in each group. So, $\frac{1}{3}$ of 12 = 4

FRACTIONS

Try this one. Suppose you've got 10 tap-dancing polar bears.

Now – what is $\frac{1}{5}$ of them? Divide the 10 tap-dancing polar bears into 5 groups. Now – how many in each group?

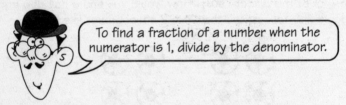

That's right. 10 divided by 5 is 2. So $\frac{1}{5}$ of 10 = 2.

To find a fraction of a number when the numerator is 1, divide by the denominator.

That's right Mr. Clevertrousers. And the good news is that now you know how to do this, finding other fractions is easy.

Let's look at how to work out $\frac{2}{3}$ of 6. Suppose we've got 6 roller-blading rabbits.

Shall we stop for lettuce soon?

First, divide the 6 roller-blading rabbits into 3 groups.

There are 2 in each group. This means that $\frac{1}{3}$ of 6 = 2. Now – here's the clever bit. We want $\frac{2}{3}$ which is 2 groups of thirds.

Which in this case is 4. So, $\frac{2}{3}$ of 6 = 4

Confused? Let's try and work out $\frac{3}{5}$ of 20.

Find $\frac{1}{5}$ by dividing 20 by 5 $20 \div 5 = 4$

So, each group has 4 things in it.

Find $\frac{3}{5}$ by working out how many are in 3 groups.

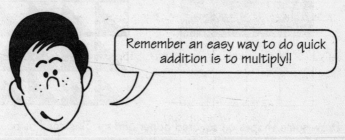

Remember an easy way to do quick addition is to multiply!!

$4 \times 3 = 12$ (or 3×4 – remember they are the same.)

You could also add up if you wanted of course because multiplying is multiple addition, like this $4 + 4 + 4 = 12$

So, $\frac{3}{5}$ of 20 = 12

FRACTIONS

Now try these. Don't be afraid to use blocks or things to help you divide into groups.

1. $\frac{1}{4}$ of 24　　　2. $\frac{3}{4}$ of 8

3. $\frac{4}{5}$ of 25　　　4. $\frac{1}{7}$ of 14

Pictures can help a lot with fractions too, so pick your favourite and draw.

NOW IT'S TIME TO PLAY LAUGH AS YOU HALVE

How many different ways can you colour in $\frac{1}{2}$ of this shape?

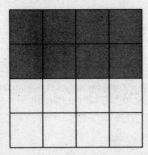 

Draw some shapes on squared paper and try. This one has been done for you in two different ways!!

JUST FOR FUN!

Try making grids of different sizes and colour in halves, thirds or quarters!

I've coloured in a third of this shape.

Now the quiz where you can . . .

USE CHOCOLATE CAKE TO ESTIMATE

Remember how important estimating is?

Well, this quiz is estimating with fractions and if you always think about the actual size of the fraction, you will get much better at fractions tests. Think of the fraction on a number line if you want, or think about chocolate cake. It might help to imagine the cake has chocolate buttons around the edge. Which number is the closest to the answer? Remember you are estimating only. Don't worry about an exact calculation.

1. Is $\frac{2}{3}$ of 16 about 24 or about 10?
2. Is $\frac{2}{4}$ of 18 about 20 or about 10?
3. Is $\frac{2}{3}$ of 21 nearer to 15 or 20?
4. Is $\frac{4}{8}$ of 100 nearer to 49 or 80?
5. Is $\frac{4}{100}$ of 99 nearer to 2 or 50?
6. Is $\frac{4}{5}$ of 100 nearer to 15 or 80?

Now watch your pulse. . .

TRUE OR FALSE ?

Just answer T for true or F for false.

1. $\frac{1}{2}$ is the same size as $\frac{50}{100}$.
2. $\frac{3}{3}$ is the same as $\frac{6}{6}$.
3. $\frac{6}{12}$ is the same size as $\frac{1}{3}$.
4. If you divide a pizza equally into ten pieces each bit is called a tenth.
5. 2 is $\frac{2}{3}$ of 16.
6. $\frac{5}{10}$ of 50 is 25.

COLIN'S CHALKBOARD CONCLUSIONS

1. Fractions are only fractions if they are equal pieces.

2. If the numerator is one then the bigger the denominator, the smaller the fraction.

3. To find a fraction of a number when the numerator is 1, divide by the denominator.

And don't forget that tenths are very important. Remember that for the next two chapters.

If I cut a cake into twenty two pieces would each bit be called a twenty-tooth? Ha ha!

Yes, you could say that, or a twenty-second.

I'll stick to twenty-tooth.

What on Earth is Place Value?

So, what on earth is place value??

> Something to do with the price of fish?

> *PLAICE GOOD VALUE*

No – look – let's try this – what's the biggest number you can think of?

> Er . . . nine million, nine hundred and ninety-nine.

OK. Do you know how to write that number as well as say it?

> Er . . . no.

Well, we all know how to write smaller numbers like twenty-five.

> That's easy. It's like this.

That's right, it's written like that because we have 2 tens and 5 units. The numbers have to go in the right columns. We can show it like this:

Tens	Units
2	5

Or you can use an abacus.

tens   units

2   5

PLACE VALUE

I expect you already knew that. Bigger numbers are just as easy to write as long as you know what the headings of your columns should be.

You can't do that Steven! They already have names, and you need to learn them. Here they are; you will need to remember up to one million.

Millions Hundred thousands Ten thousands Thousands Hundreds Tens Units

I know it seems like a lot to learn – but the easy way to work them out is to know each column is 10 times bigger than the last one, starting with the units column. Look at this;

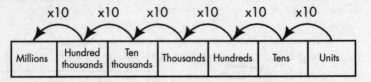

So, if you forget what column comes next, write them out, beginning with Units and make each column 10 times bigger. If you can't remember the easy way to make a number 10 times bigger, here it is again:

3 times 10 is 30. You just add a zero. 20 times 10 is 200. You add a zero. So what is 13 multiplied by 10?

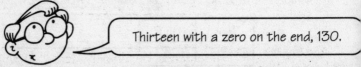

Thirteen with a zero on the end, 130.

Great! You see, you've remembered already. The numbers move to the left.

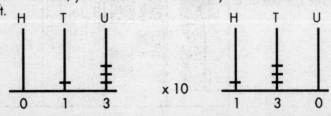

Now all we need to do is try out our skills with some really big numbers.

Let's try putting TWO THOUSAND, FOUR HUNDRED AND SEVENTY-THREE into the correct columns.

We can write this another way to make it slightly easier.

> 2 thousand
> 4 hundred
> 70
> 3

Read that out loud to check that it is the same number we started with.

OK. First, ask yourself:

1. How many thousands have I got?   2
2. How many hundreds have I got?   4
3. How many tens have I got?   7
4. How many units have I got?   3

Now let's put those numbers into our columns to find out what it looks like:

Millions	Hundred thousands	Ten thousands	Thousands	Hundreds	Tens	Units
			2	4	7	3

On an abacus,
it looks like this:

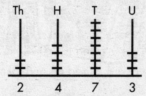

        Th   H   T   U

        2   4   7   3

And like this, with
base ten blocks:

Thousands	Hundreds	Tens	Units

Now let's try to put sixty thousand, four hundred and two in columns. Watch out for the zeros.

Millions	Hundred thousands	Ten thousands	Thousands	Hundreds	Tens	Units
		6	0	4	0	2

It would look like this.

BE A WHIZZ AT THIS QUIZ

Try to put these numbers in columns.

1. ten thousand, six hundred and forty-two
2. two hundred and twenty-seven thousand, eight hundred and fifteen
3. fifteen thousand and four

Those were quite hard so don't be afraid to take a peek at the answers and see where the different numbers go!

Always make sure your column headings are correct and that your numbers go in the right columns.

Sometimes you are asked to add on and take away from very big numbers.

There's no need to panic. If you can remember the easy ways to add on and take away from smaller numbers in the first section of this book, then this bit will be easy! Suppose you are asked to add on a number. First think:

Which column does this number go in?

Then just make that column bigger by the amount you have to add on.

Er ... what?

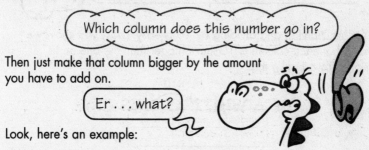

Look, here's an example:

Say you want to add 10 on to 6,754 (six thousand, seven hundred and fifty-four).

Well, you need to add on one 10, so the tens column goes up by one, like this:

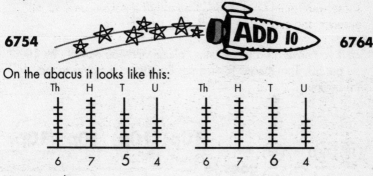

6754 ADD 10 **6764**

On the abacus it looks like this:

Th	H	T	U		Th	H	T	U
6	7	5	4		6	7	6	4

Here's another:

Add on 400 to 8,213 (eight thousand, two hundred and thirteen).

I need to make my hundreds column bigger by 4 like this:

8213 ADD 400 **8613**

Impress your friends!! Practise adding on to really big numbers so that you can amaze people with your huge brain!!

Multiplying and dividing by ten

Is there anything easy about place value?

Yes. Multiplying and dividing by 10 is easy. Look, you know we said that each column is 10 times bigger than the one on its right? It works like this.

×10

Hundreds	Tens	Units
		8	×10

The hundreds are 10 times bigger than the tens, and the tens are 10 times bigger than the units.

Hundreds	Tens	Units
	8	0

So, if you have an 8 in the units column and you multiply by 10, you get 80. That means 8 tens, not 8 units, so it moves to the tens column.

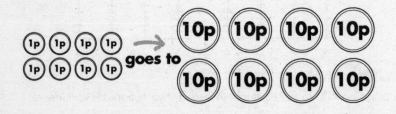

Now suppose you have 5 tens.

That's 50, isn't it?

Yes, well done. And you want to divide the 50 by 10. The 5 moves out of the tens column and into the units column.

50 ÷ 10 is 5

Hundreds	Tens	Units
	5	0

÷ 10

Hundreds	Tens	Units
		5

So if you had 50 sweets to share between 10 people they would get 5 each. Try these.

1. 94 x 10 =   2. 940 ÷ 10 =
3. 59 x 10 =   4. 590 ÷ 10 =

PLACE VALUE MOT

Look how important zeros are.

Write these numbers in words.

1. 400,000
2. 4,000,000
3. 1,234,567
4.

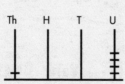

5.

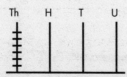

6. What is the value of the 6 here?

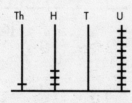

PLACE VALUE

7. What is the value of the 6 here?

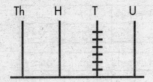

8. What is the value of the 6 here?

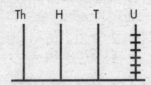

9. If you were saving up for a bike, would you rather have this many pounds, or this many?

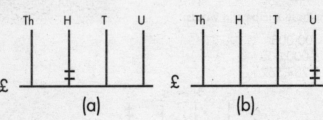

How much is:

10. 62 x 10 =
11. 650 ÷ 10 =
12. Make 9 ten times bigger.

Play the Place Value Game on page 132 for more practice.

COLIN'S CHALKBOARD CONCLUSIONS

1. Make sure you get the numbers in the right columns.

2. Each column is ten times larger than the one to the right.

3. Zero is a very important number.

Right – I've got all my columns – where do I get the numbers from?

Ah, that's not what I meant, Steven.

Do I need to Know about
Decimals?

Decimals are really important. They're used all around us all the time such as when we

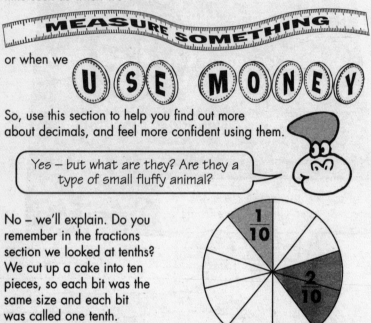

MEASURE SOMETHING

or when we

USE MONEY

So, use this section to help you find out more about decimals, and feel more confident using them.

> Yes – but what are they? Are they a type of small fluffy animal?

No – we'll explain. Do you remember in the fractions section we looked at tenths? We cut up a cake into ten pieces, so each bit was the same size and each bit was called one tenth. Two bits were two tenths.

$\frac{1}{10}$

$\frac{2}{10}$

Well – decimals are all to do with tenths and lots of tenths.

> Decimals and fractions are very closely linked.

Try this on your calculator.

Key in $1 \div 2 =$ and you get 0.5.

This means that when you divide one whole cake into two equal bits, each bit is a half. A half in decimals is 0.5.

You say it like this: 'zero point five.'

Most calculators can't write fractions as $\frac{1}{5}$ (a fifth) or $\frac{1}{4}$ (a quarter). Calculators like working with decimals.

Mmm.

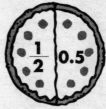

Have you noticed that you can write fractions like divisions, such as $1 \div 6$, or you can write them like fractions, e.g. $\frac{1}{6}$?

Now play around with your calculator for a bit. Key in these fractions: 5 over 10 and 6 over 12.

$\frac{5}{10}$ (key in 5 ÷ 10)   or $\frac{6}{12}$ or $\frac{4}{8}$ or $\frac{12}{24}$

Hey! Look what happens! They're all the same!

Now play the 'Three in a Row' game in the games section.

Now let's get back to decimals. In the last section we looked at place value and columns.

But!

. . . we only looked at numbers bigger than 1. We know now that some numbers (like fractions) are smaller than 1 whole one. So, we need to add an extra column to show people when we are talking about numbers less than 1, like this:

DECIMALS

Tens	Units (one whole one)	•	Tenths

Who ordered ten pizzas?

Can't think!

Now we have a column to help us show numbers less than 1. Let's say that I had $\frac{1}{10}$ of a pizza. Instead of writing it as a fraction we can make it look much neater by writing it as a decimal.

One tenth of a pizza would only be about one bite.

Yes, a whole pizza divided into ten equal bits makes tenths. You put the one tenth in the tenths column like this:

Hundreds	Tens	Units	•	Tenths
		0	•	1

We use decimals to talk about numbers less than one.

So, $\frac{1}{10}$ means the same as 0.1

To say it out loud, you say: 'one tenth means the same as zero point one'.

Use your calculator and key in 1 ÷ 10 =

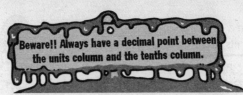

Beware!! Always have a decimal point between the units column and the tenths column.

Yes, now, remember how important zeros are? Well, there has to be a 0 in the units column if you only have tenths. Don't forget! For example, $\frac{1}{10}$ is written 0.1. So, how do you think you'd write two tenths? Try on your calculator.

Key in 2 ÷ 10 =

Hundreds	Tens	Units	•	Tenths
		0	•	2

So, $\frac{2}{10}$ = 0.2

Yes. See if you can do these.

1. $\frac{3}{10}$ =

2. $\frac{4}{10}$ =

3. $\frac{5}{10}$ =

4. $\frac{6}{10}$ =

Easy, isn't it?!!

Useful fact:
$$\frac{5}{10} = \frac{1}{2} = 0.5$$

If you have tens, units and tenths then you just have to make sure that the correct numbers go in the correct columns.

DECIMALS

Say you need to make 23 and 7 tenths which is 2 tens, 3 units and 7 tenths.

> Mmm. 23 whole pizzas and almost another whole one.

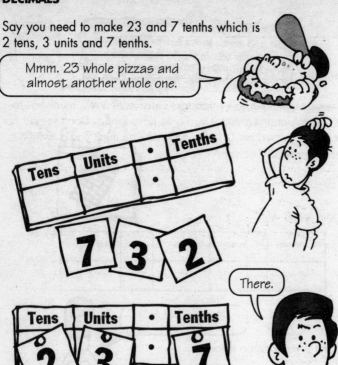

GUESSABLE DECIMALS!

See if you can write these as decimals:

1. $15\frac{3}{10}$

2. $28\frac{1}{10}$

3. $31\frac{9}{10}$

4. $45\frac{8}{10}$

MEGA TRICKY GUESSABLE DECIMALS!

Can you be really clever and work out for yourself what these would look like as decimals?

1. $147\frac{5}{10}$

2. $176\frac{2}{10}$

3. $1563\frac{9}{10}$

4. $17653\frac{7}{10}$

The column on the right side of the decimal point is tenths.

But when we see prices of things there are always 2 numbers after the decimal point like this:

This is because there is another column on the right of the tenths. This is called the hundredths. Look – it's like this:

Hundreds	Tens	Units	•	Tenths	Hundredths
		7	•	8	

Yes. But what are hundredths?

Think back to fractions!! One hundredth is $\frac{1}{100}$.

So a hundredth of a pizza would be like just one olive.

Yes that's right – about that. Now, look, Horace is holding up a number.

Twenty-six point nine six. In money we say twenty-six pounds and ninety-six pence. Can you work out which column will hold which number?

Tens	Units	.	Tenths	Hundredths
2	6	.	9	6

The 2 goes in the tens column. The 6 are pounds and they go in the units column. The 90 pence goes in the tenths of a pound column.

That's because it's nine tenths of a pound.

And the 6 pence goes in the hundredths column.

We need two columns to show pence in money. That's because pennies are less than one whole pound. And one penny is one hundredth of a pound because you need a hundred of them to make one pound.

AMAZE YOUR FRIENDS!!

Changing pence to pounds and pence is easy. Look carefully at where the decimal point goes in all of these.

216p = £2.16   367p = £3.67   498p = £4.98

Can you see that the decimal point always goes before the last two numbers? The last two numbers are the pennies, so 345p = £3.45. It's 3 whole pounds (three hundred of the pennies) then 4 ten pences and 5 pence.

Tens (£10)	Units (pounds)	.	Tens (10 pences)	Hundredths (pennies)
	£1 £1 £1	.	10p 10p 10p 10p	1p 1p 1p 1p 1p

£ 3 · 4 5

Having the decimal point and then two more numbers always works no matter how big your first number is. Look at this one:

456,789p = £4,567.89

That is four thousand, five hundred and sixty-seven pounds, then the decimal point before the eighty-nine pennies.

Remember how important zeros are? Well, it is the same if one of the columns has a zero:

3,403p = £34.03   100,010p = £1,000.10
Thirty-four pounds and three pence.   One thousand pounds and ten pence.

And now here's a really easy bit.

Putting the decimal point before the last two numbers works in exactly the same way for metres and centimetres, because there are 100 cm in a metre.

123 cm   = 1.23 m
451 cm   = 4.51 m
5,673 cm = 56.73 m
1,205 cm = 12.05 m
5,940 cm = 59.40 m

Practise doing these really quickly and then race an adult!!

Don't forget to write the correct unit of measure. Some are money and some are length.

1. 87,654,321p   2. 3,456,789 cm   3. 1,234,567,890 cm
4. 9,870,003p   5. 6,700p   6. 800,000 cm

Multiplying and dividing by ten

Remember multiplying and dividing by ten in the place value chapter and also in the multiplying and dividing chapters? It's easy. Look back if you've forgotten. (See pages 47 and 90.)

It is just as easy to do it with decimals. The same thing happens. Look at these multiplications by 10.

Look closely at the headings to the columns. $\frac{1}{10}$ means the same as one tenth.

10s	1s	•	$\frac{1}{10}$s	$\frac{1}{100}$s
	7	•	8	

×10

10s	1s	•	$\frac{1}{10}$s	$\frac{1}{100}$s
7	8	•		

7.8 seven point eight multiplied by ten is 78 and no tenths. 78.

What's happened to the decimal point? Have you lost it?

No, Steven. We don't need to put point zero, like this: 78.0. We could do that, but people don't usually bother.

100s	10s	1s	•	$\frac{1}{10}$ s	$\frac{1}{100}$ s	
	4	9	•	7	9	×10

100s	10s	1s	•	$\frac{1}{10}$ s	$\frac{1}{100}$ s	
4	9	7	•	9		÷10

49.79 x 10 is 497.9. Again, everything moves one column to the left and you get 497.9. You could write 497.90 if you wanted to.

Dividing any number by 10 is just as easy. To divide 497.90 by 10, everything moves one column to the right.

I know what's going to happen! It is going to end up where it started! You said that division undoes multiplication so we end up with . . . er . . . whatever it was.

Yes, exactly. 49.79

100s	10s	1s	•	$\frac{1}{10}$ s	$\frac{1}{100}$ s
	4	9	•	7	9

GUZZLE AT THIS PUZZLE

Try these.

1. 93.8 x 10 =   2. 938.0 ÷ 10 =
3. 45.1 ÷ 10 =   4. 4.51 x 10 =
5. 9,562.09 x 10 =   6. 95,620.9 ÷ 10 =

Can you see the pattern?

IT'S RUDE TO POINT, BUT NOT IN THIS QUIZ

1. Add 345p and 355p and write your answer as a decimal.
2. Five pounds and eighty pence add £2.70.
3. Draw the columns we use for whole numbers and decimals and put on the names, starting with hundreds on the left and ending with hundredths on the right. Don't forget the decimal point.
4. Write a half as a decimal.
5. Write three and four tenths as a decimal.

IT'S EXTREMELY RUDE TO POINT, BUT NOT IN THIS ADVANCED QUIZ FOR BRAINBOXES

1. Write this number in words: 7.98.
2. How many hundredths in the hundredths column in this number: 7.98?
3. How many tenths in the tenths column in 7.98?
4. How many whole ones in 7.98?
5. 83.90 multiplied by 10.

CHALLENGE

Number lines, fractions and decimals.

Draw a number line zero to 4. Put on 0.5 like this.

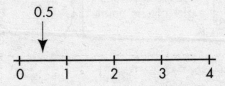

Now put on $1\frac{1}{2}$, 2.5, 3.5 and 3.9.

COLIN'S CHALKBOARD CONCLUSIONS

1. Decimals and fractions are very closely linked.

2. We use decimals to talk about numbers less than one.

3. We put a decimal point between the whole numbers and the tenths.

4. The column on the right of the units and the other side of the decimal point is tenths.

THIS WAY TO THE POINT

No – Steven I said put the TENTHS to the right of the point.

Where's the Button on My
Calculator
for Pizza?

Look — the batteries have run out.

The key thing is to get good at using a calculator.

Key thing? That's almost a joke! Key thing!

Yes — all right Steven. Now — whatever you do, don't use a calculator when you don't need to. It might make your brain rot. And it takes up too much time anyway. Look at these two calculations:

1. 100 + 100 + 100 + 100 + 100 would take ages to key in, but you can see quickly that the answer is 500.

2. 4,000,000,000 (four hundred million) take away 1.

Not only is that too long to put into the calculator, but you can work it out in your head much quicker anyway. Just think back to the chapter about place value (page 85). The answer is 399,999,999. Three hundred and ninety-nine million, nine hundred and ninety-nine thousand, nine hundred and ninety-nine!

Remember: it is very easy to press the wrong key when you use a calculator.

IMPRESS YOUR FRIENDS

This is how to impress your friends by getting really quick at keying numbers into the calculator.

First, key in 123 x 45.

Practise doing it, then try again with your eyes shut.

Now try to do this quiz with your calculator as fast as you can. Write down your starting time, then just write down the answers.

A GLUTTON FOR BUTTONS

1. 48 ÷ 12   =
2. 123 + 456   =
3. 789 – 123   =
4. 120 x 120   =
5. 160 x 160   =
6. 111 ÷ 3   =
7. 111 x 7   =
8. 2,345 – 1,234 =
9. 1.04 x 2   =
10. 1.25 ÷ 5   =

Look back to the section on decimals if the answers to those last two blows your mind.

Check your answers and look back at the questions and see if there are any you could have done much quicker in your head. Number 7 maybe?

Tomorrow, try to do these again and be much quicker. Don't use the calculator if you know the answer. That will make you much quicker.

NOW CHALLENGE A FRIEND OR AN
ADULT TO A RACE AND DO IT AGAIN.

OK, now shut your eyes and see
if you have a picture of the keys
in your head. This is going to help
you to press the right key and
be very quick at keying in.

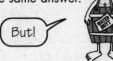

Beware-
The order
matters.

Sometimes in maths the order doesn't matter such as
4 x 5 and 5 x 4. These both give the same answer.

But!

. . . sometimes the order does matter. 5 ÷ 3 is very different
from 3 ÷ 5. Mathematicians put brackets around bits of
equations to be done first. (Look back to page 30.)

Now which kind of calculator do you have? Look at this equation:

1+ (2 x 6) =

Mathematicians put a bracket around the 2 x 6 because it is a rule
of maths that multiplication is done before addition. Some calculators
know this!

Yeah – I knew that. It's easy.

They do 1 + (2 x 6) by doing the bracket first – even if we don't
tell them that!

2 x 6 is 12. Then you add the one. 1 + 12 = 13.

CALCULATORS

But other calculators (usually those for small children) will do the equation in the order you put it in.

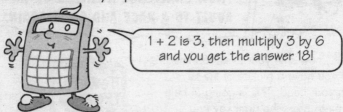

1 + 2 is 3, then multiply 3 by 6 and you get the answer 18!

Try out the sum yourself. If your calculator gives the answer 18, you will need to save up for the more advanced kind.

Ways to be not just quick but also brilliant at using a calculator.

Step 1

Always estimate first. Try this.

123 x 25

This is quite a hard sum to do in your head, but you can still estimate.

First, look at the numbers. One hundred lots of 25 would be 2,500 (twenty-five hundred or two thousand, five hundred) but that is too few. Two hundred lots of 25 would be 5,000 (fifty hundred or five thousand) and that is too much. So the answer you are looking for is somewhere between those two numbers.

So if you key in the sum and you get the answer 4, you know you are wrong somewhere.

If you key it in and get three million (3,000,000) you will also know you are wrong.

Think about which keys you press. Remember that thousands of people make mistakes on calculators because they press the wrong key.

So key in 123 x 25 = very carefully.

Always check what you did. If you got 3,075, ask yourself if this is about the answer you were expecting. Is it between 2,500 and 5,000?

Hey – it is.

Good. If you get a wrong answer, go back and try to work out what you did wrong and try again.

If you think you are right, to be quite sure check your answer. The easiest way to do that is to key it in again.

or

Start with the 3,075 in your answer and check by using the opposite operation – in this case division. Remember from the earlier chapters? Look at page 48 if you've forgotten.

3,075 ÷ 25 should get you back to 123.

Estimating

Estimating is very important whatever maths you are doing. Try this one. 999,999,999 x 123,456,789. Make a guess at the answer. Too hard?

Looks way too hard.

And it is too big to go in the calculator. Try this. Ask yourself what is an easy number very near 999,999,999.

1,000,000,000

(a thousand million, which is called a billion in America and France)

Yes. And you know how easy it is to multiply by numbers with zeros in them. Look back at page 47 if you've forgotten.

CALCULATORS

123,456,789 multiplied by a thousand million would have 9 zeros just like a thousand million has 9 zeros.

123,456,789,000,000,000

Now try to do it on the calculator. Can you see the E that appears? That means there is an error in the answer on the screen.

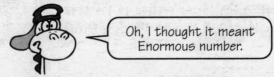

Oh, I thought it meant Enormous number.

So, can you make an estimate for 999,999 × 123,456,789? The answer must be very close to 12,356,789,000,000. *

OK – let's move on – now do you know about the calculator constant?

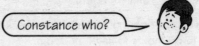

Constance who?

Constant not Constance! Well – calculators vary a bit. This is terribly annoying, but try this on yours. Key in 10 + + then = = = =

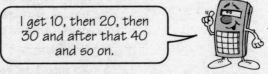

I get 10, then 20, then 30 and after that 40 and so on.

Right, play around with yours until it does that. Hopefully you will see a K appear on your screen.

K? Constant begins with a 'C'! Can't these mathematicians spell?!

Now, try these:

40 – – = = =
5 x x = = =
6 ÷ ÷ = = = =

Useful eh?

* Answer is 123,456,665,543,211

110

It certainly is. Got a real problem table? How about 7 times?

Key in 7 ++ === and say the numbers as you press the = key. If you do that 7 times every day for 7 days, that's 49 times. Then impress your friends!

Try the decimals and fractions 3 in a Row game in the games section at the back. Practise it and then challenge a friend.

Square numbers

What are square numbers?

Numbers that are boring like Colin?

Have a look at this number pattern that lots of people know. You get the numbers from making squares like this:

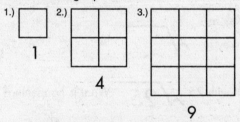

1.) 1 2.) 4 3.) 9

WHERE'S THE SQUARE?

Try these:
1. What would the fourth and fifth numbers be, above?
2. What would the tenth number be?
3. Do you think that multiplying 12 by 12 would give you a squared number?

These numbers are called square numbers.
Do you see?

Square numbers are numbers that can be made into squares.

CALCULATORS

What's the biggest square number?

That is a silly question – they go on for ever, because numbers go on for ever, but you could challenge a friend to find a bigger square number than you can.

The square root key

On the calculator, to get back to the length of the side of the square, you can use the square root key that looks like this.

Try this. Key in:

16. Now key in $\sqrt{}$

Now try it with 25. $\sqrt{25}$ What is happening?

Let's look at the first one. Now – remember 16 is a square number. $4 \times 4 = 16$. So the square root key gets a square number back to the start, the length of the side of the square.

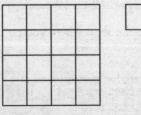

$4 \times 4 = 16$ $\sqrt{16} = 4$

Just Mucking About Quiz

Find some huge square numbers such as 17 x 17 and 99 x 99.

Challenge yourself to learn all the square numbers up to 12 x 12, or even up to 25 x 25.

> Consecutive numbers are numbers next to each other like 3, 4, 5.

Multiply together three consecutive numbers such as 6 x 7 x 8 = 336 to make the following:

1. 6
2. A number over 200 but smaller than 250.
3. A number as close as you can get to 500.
4. A number as near as you can get to 1,000.

Did you think that your answers to question 4 might be double your answers for 3? That's good mathematical thinking, but I expect you can see why that doesn't work.

Other keys on the calculator

% Look in the next chapter on percentages.

M This is the memory key.

Unfortunately calculators are so varied that to find out how to use this key you need to look at the information sheet for your calculator, which you have probably lost.

Either

1. Speak very politely to the shop where you bought it and ask for a copy.
2. Write to the manufacturers.
3. Smile at your maths teacher and ask them to explain.
4. This is the easiest – play around with your calculator until you can see what it is doing.

CoLiN's CHALKBOARD CONCLUSIONS

1. Always estimate first.
2. Think about which keys you press.
3. Always check what you did. Did you get the answer you were expecting? If not, work out what you did wrong and try again.
4. Play around with numbers on your calculator and think about what you are doing; it can help you to get much better at maths.
5. Don't use a calculator for things you can do in your head!
6. Calculators can do much more than check what you do, or do big sums for you. They can help you to think like real mathematicians.

I'd really like a calculator with chocolate buttons.

Percentages
are 99% Impossible

Percentages can seem really hard and it's normally because people think that they are completely different to anything they have done before. Actually, if you followed the work in the fractions and decimals sections you'll find that percentages can be a doddle!!

Percentages are all about hundredths or $\frac{1}{100}$.

See the fractions section if you can't remember what that means!

This square is split into 100 equal pieces, just like a normal 100 square.

Hey – over here – I've found some shade.

There are 10 squares shaded in, so 10 out of 100 are shaded. The fraction would look like this:

$\frac{10}{100}$

The words 'per cent' mean 'out of 100'.

That's the beginning of the word 'percentage'.

PERCENTAGES

Exactly. So if we have 10 out of 100 shaded we can say that we have 10 per cent. It's written like this:

10 % or $\frac{10}{100}$

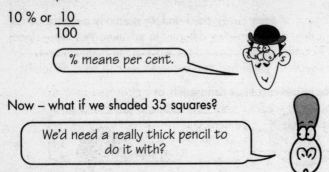

% means per cent.

Now – what if we shaded 35 squares?

We'd need a really thick pencil to do it with?

Yes, that's not quite what we meant Steven. What percentage would we have? Come on – let's do it in steps.

 Step 1

What fraction have I got? $\frac{35}{100}$

 **Step 2**

What is this in words?   35 out of 100

 Step 3

What is this as a percentage?   35 %

Now you can see how easy it is, try these.

Always put it as a fraction out of 100 first and look at the numerator (the top number). This will give you your percentage.

Write the fraction and the percentage.

1.   48 squares shaded
2.   99 squares shaded
3.   65 squares shaded
4.   50 squares shaded

A percentage must come from a fraction that has 100 as the denominator (the bottom number). The numerator (top number) of the fraction is your percentage.

Where have you heard the words 'percentage' or 'per cent' the most? Probably at school where your teachers sometimes give you your test results as a percentage.

So, which is better 50% or 99%?

'Better' is a funny word isn't it? What he should have asked was, 'Which is more, 50% or 99%?'

Well, let's have a look at which is bigger. To do that we need our hundred square again.

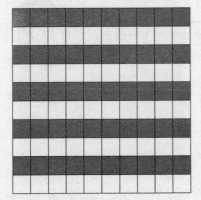

50 squares coloured in
50% of squares coloured in

99 squares coloured in
99% of squares coloured in

One hundred square has 50 squares coloured in, so that's 50% and the other has 99 squares coloured in which is 99%. Which hundred square has the most small squares coloured in? That's right, the second one. So, we can see that 99% is bigger. In fact 99% is nearly a whole one, so if you got that in a test you would be doing really well!!!

PERCENTAGES

Percentages of a number

You'll often need to find out a percentage of a number.

Zelda needs to take 50% off the original price of the T-shirt to find out how much it is now. There are a few steps we need to do:

Find out what 50% of the original price is.

Take that away from the original price.

Wooow! Hang on. I don't know how to do step one yet!

Don't panic. It isn't as difficult as you might think. There are some percentages that can easily be written as other fractions.

See if you can remember these!

$$50\% = \frac{50}{100} = \frac{1}{2}$$

$$25\% = \frac{25}{100} = \frac{1}{4}$$

$$10\% = \frac{10}{100} = \frac{1}{10}$$

$$1\% = \frac{1}{100} \quad \text{(read that as one hundredth)}$$

So, find out the fraction of the price and this will be your percentage!

See the fractions section if you have forgotten how to find a fraction of a number.

Let's have a look at that T-shirt again.

Remember, was to find 50% of the original price. We're going to change this to a fraction. And 50% is the same as $\frac{1}{2}$. So find $\frac{1}{2}$ of the original price because this is easier.

 What is $\frac{1}{2}$ of £10?

£10 ÷ 2 = £5

Exactly. Now . . .

Step 2 Take that away from the original price £10 − £5 = £5

I only need to pay £5 for the T-shirt instead of £10. I love sales.

Here's another.

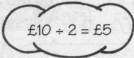

Step 1 What is 25% of £20?

Change this to a fraction. Remember how to divide the top and bottom of a fraction by the same number? 25% is $\frac{25}{100}$ as a fraction. $\frac{25 \div 25}{100 \div 25} = \frac{1}{4}$ So what is $\frac{1}{4}$ of £20?

 It's £5

Step 2 Take that away from the original price. £20 − £5 = £15

That bag now costs £15.

BARGAIN JARGON

Find the new sale prices of these items.

1. 10% OFF LABEL PRICE — £10

2. SALE 50% OFF — VASE £30

3. TRAINERS 25% OFF — £40

4. ALL JEANS 20% OFF MARKED PRICE — £50

A clue Watson! Over here. Quick!

CLUE: 20% is 2 lots of 10%

So far we have only looked at things going down in price but sometimes things go up too. The steps are almost the same as before. In fact, only changes. Look:

 Find the percentage of your original price.

Remember, change the percentage to an easy fraction if you can!!

 Add that amount to the original price.

Can you see the difference?

Look, here's an example of percentage increase:

 RADIO PRICES GONE UP BY 10%

 £80

Suppose we wanted to know what is 10% of £80. First we change the percentage to an easy fraction. 10% changes to $\frac{1}{10}$. Now what is $\frac{1}{10}$ of £80?. That's £8.

 Add this on to your original price. £80 + £8 = £88

So, the new price of the radio is £88.

> If you are taking a percentage off something you take away from the original amount.

If you are adding a percentage onto something you add on to your original amount.

A DIFFICULT BIT!!!!

Sometimes you need to find a percentage of something that is not an easy fraction. Suppose Colin wants to buy this moose and the label says it has 15% off.

What's an easy way to work this out?

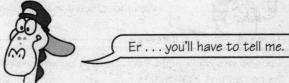

> Er . . . you'll have to tell me.

OK. First you split 15% into 10% + 5%.
Then you find out what 10% is. $\frac{1}{10}$ of £10 = £1

Notice we changed the 10% into a fraction!

Then you find out what 5% is.

5% is one half of 10% because 5 is half of 10.

5% of £10 = £0.50 (or 50p)

Then, and here's the clever bit, add those two amounts together to give you 15%. (10% + 5% is 15%).

So £1 + £0.50 = £1.50

So, Colin needs to take £1.50 off the original price of the moose. He will have to pay: £10 – £1.50 = £8.50

This way of splitting up percentages works for other numbers too.

30% = 3 lots of 10%
45% = 4 lots of 10% + 5%

You could even find 1% of something this way. Can you think how? What about finding 10% first? That is usually easy. Then what could you do?

I know. Find a tenth of that!

Exactly. Well done. Now we move on to:

Using a calculator

Can I use my calculator to find out percentages?

Yes, you can! You might have a button on your calculator that has the percentage sign on it.

%

Here's how you can use this to find 15% of £10.

1		0		X		1		5		%		=

You should get 1.5 and as this is pounds, the answer is £1.50.

QUICKIES FOR QUICK KEYS

How fast can you get using the calculator? Try these as a
timed challenge.

1. 40% of 50
2. 75% of 120
3. 18% of 60
4. 35% of 60

This next bit is quite hard.

What your calculator is actually doing when it is working out 15% of
£10 is this:

$\frac{15}{100}$ of £10

Remember that means 15% of £10.

It works out like this:

15 divided by 100 times 10.
15 ÷ 100 x 10 =

When you see the word 'of' in a calculation it often means
multiply   e.g. ½ of 6 is ½ x 6 = 3. Try this out and see.

Try those four questions from the last page again. But this time try doing them like the calculator.

Question 1 is 40 over 100 (that means 40 divided by 100) of 50, and you get the answer 20.

REALLY VERY MEGA DIFFICULT BIT

DANGER: Do Not Look At This If Your Knees Are Wobbling

This is what you can do if you get really horrible numbers and no calculator. Let's suppose that you had to find out 1% of £200.

OK. Hang in there. Now, you need to find out what 1 divided by 100 is, so that you can then multiply that by 200.

$$\frac{1}{100} = 0.01$$

$$0.01 \times 200 = £2$$

If you are feeling bold, try to work out 17% of £38 the same way.

$$\frac{17}{100} \times 38 = £6.46$$

Use a calculator if you want on sums like this. You can do the ÷ and the x in any order here, and you'll get the same answer.

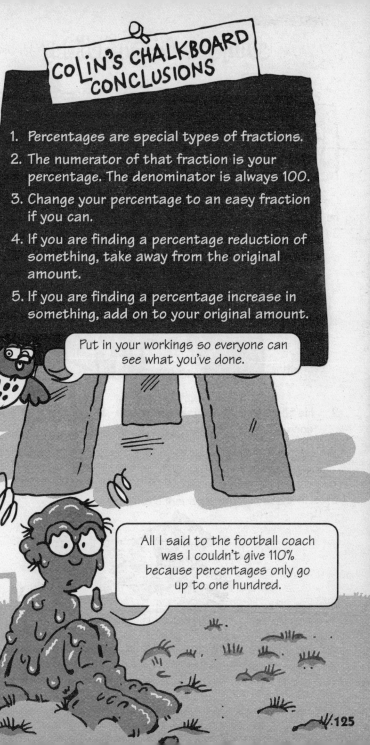

Colin Jets Off on Holiday

Colin is off to France and then America with his dad and Callum, but he has too much luggage. He can only take a total of 30 kilograms on the plane. Which bags can he take?

1.

   c 15.48 kg

   d 28.70 kg

   a 19.10 kg

   b 13.50 kg

   e 11.90 kg

2. He changes £20 to American dollars ($). He gets 1.7 dollars for each pound. How many dollars does he get?

3. How many francs does he get when he changes £20 to francs at 8.6 francs for each pound?

4. He sees sweets for sale in the airport.

   £1.30 for 10. How much for 1? How much for 2?

5. He is bored on the plane so the flight attendant tells him he has 4500 more kilometres to go. A mile is about 1.5 km (actually 1.600 metres). Roughly how far is there to go in miles?

6. In France he sees a cool sweatshirt and wonders if he can persuade his dad to buy it for him. How much is it?

7. In America he sees a computer game for sale for $10. He knows that in Britain this game costs £12. Is it cheaper in America? Work out how much £12 is in dollars (see q.2).

8. In the airport coming home he wants to buy a present for his mum.

How much is it?

9. Colin is bored on the plane going home and when the flight attendant asks him how old he is, Colin says he will think about it and gets his calculator out. He decides to work out how many days he has been alive!

How old are you?

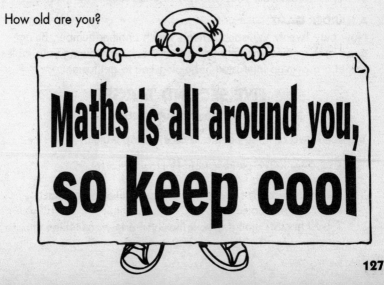

Maths is all around you, so keep cool

Games to Get Good At

For these games you need someone to play with you.

I'll play! Me!

TEN WHISPERS

This game will make you great at addition!

You need to be so quick at this game that you will amaze everyone.

You need: a partner (and a stop watch if you want).

1. Your partner says a number between 0 and 10, so you must say the number that makes it up to 10. For example your friend might say 4.
2. You reply 6 because 6 + 4 makes 10.

3. Practise this until you can reply in one second – or less!

A HARDER GAME

Now play Twenty Whispers. Then try with another number. Being good at this game will help you just as much as knowing your tables, so get a grown-up interested in helping you to get faster.

FIVE SECOND TARGET

Addition and subtraction.

You need: two or three people, a dice, a stop watch.

1. Choose a target number e.g. 30.
2. Throw a dice, say 6.
3. Within 5 seconds say the number that makes 6 up to 30.
   6 + 24 = 30. So you say 24.
4. Take it in turns until everyone has had a few goes, then choose another target number e.g. 100.

THREE NUMBER TARGET
Practise adding with big numbers.

You need: three people, pencil and paper, and a calculator ONLY if you need to sort out an argument.

1. Choose a target, say 100.
2. The first person says a number smaller than the target, say 30.
3. The second person says another number and the total, say 20, so now the total is 50.
4. The third person must say the number that makes it up to the target, 50 + 50 makes 100.

SUBTRACTION TARGET
Don't forget that taking away is the opposite of addition!

You need: two or more people, a pack of cards (ace to 9s only), pencil and paper.

1. The dealer turns over 1 card to make the tens number in the target, say a 2 so your target number is twenty something. The second card makes the units number, say 5.

    Your target is 25.
2. Give each player four cards.
3. Everyone must make a calculation with their cards to try to make a number as close to the target as possible. The cards can be used in any order.

42 − 15   67− 43

Colin has made 27   Zelda has made 24
Zelda's is closest so scores 10 points.

TABLES SPINNER
This helps with learning tables.

You need: a spinner, a paper clip and a pack of cards (ace to 10s only at first – you can use the jack as 11 later). To make a spinner, draw a circle on paper and divide it into as many sections as you want.

This spinner has space for each times tables from 2 times to 11 times. You could just have the tables that are giving you trouble e.g. 6, 7 and 9 times.

Hold the paper clip on the central dot with the point of the pencil and spin the clip with your finger.

1. Spin the spinner and take a card, these are your factor numbers and you multiply them together. So, if you spin 4 and take a 6 card, 4 x 6 is 24.
2. Score 24 and the first person to get over 200 (or choose a winning number) wins – and this is a time when it would be good to use a calculator.

LOWEST SCORE SPLODGE
This is good for learning tables, too.

You need: pencil and paper, two or three people, two dice.

1. Draw these splodges on paper.

2. Take turns to throw both dice and total the numbers e.g. 5 + 6 is 11.
3. If your number is a factor of a splodge, cross that splodge out

and score zero. (So you could cross out 55 because 11 is a
factor of 55.)

4. If there is no splodge with your total as a factor you score 20.
    Lowest score wins.

SUPER HARD GAME

Score $33\frac{1}{3}$ when there is no splodge with your total as a factor. (Your
score will be easier than you think, $33\frac{1}{3}$, $66\frac{2}{3}$, 100, $133\frac{1}{3}$
and so on.)

SUPER MEGA HARD GAME

This time score the splodge number. Keep a total of these. Highest
score wins. (This would be a good time to use a calculator.)

DECIMAL THREE IN A ROW
This uses fractions, decimals and a whole lot of estimating.

You need: a calculator, a partner, two different coloured pens, pencil
and paper.

Draw a number line from 0 to 1 (so all the numbers in this game are
going to be less than 1, just like lots of the numbers in the
fractions and decimal chapters).

If you want, you can mark in some of the numbers. You can put in
0.5 easily because that is half way along. When you have played
the game a few times, don't do this marking.

1. Choose two numbers between 1 and 19 to make a fraction.
    Write your fraction down with the smaller number on top
    (otherwise you will forget it and you might lose the game). If
    you chose 2 and 17 your fraction will look like this.

    $$\frac{2}{17}$$

2. Now turn that into a decimal on the calculator.
    Key in $2 \div 17 = 0.117647$.

If you get a number larger than 1 you
have gone wrong somewhere.

3. Now put that number on the line with your colour of pen.

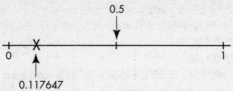

4. Now the next person has a go. You can use any of the numbers 1–19 as often as you want. Suppose they choose 4 and 8. They key in 4 ÷ 8 = and get 0.5 (Do you remember that is a half? You did that in the decimals chapter.) So they put one of their colour marks half way along.
5. Now you get to the clever bit. The aim of the game is to get 3 of your marks in a row with none of your partner's marks between any of yours. So you want one really near to your 0.1176 that you had last time. So which numbers could you choose?

Last time you did 2 ÷ 17 = 0.117647.
How could you make that a tiny bit larger or smaller?
Go on taking turns like this until someone has 3 in a row.

TRICKY 24s
This is good for multiplication and other rules.

You need: any number of players and a pack of cards (make the Jack 11, Queen 12 etc).

1. Lay down nine cards on the table.
2. Take turns to choose any of the cards to make the number 24 in any way you want but you must include multiplication, e.g. with the 11 and a 2 you can do (11 x 2) + 2 to make 24. (Always do the brackets first.)
3. That player keeps the cards and scores 2. Lowest score wins, so use the fewest cards possible.
4. Replace the two cards on the table with others from the pack.

PLACE VALUE GAME
This is about putting numbers in columns.

You need: two or more people, some playing cards (numbers 1 to 9 only plus one picture card to represent 0), some paper and a pencil.

1. On your paper each draw some place value columns going up to thousands to start with. As you get better at the game you could use bigger numbers. Lay the cards face down onto the table.

2. Each player takes it in turn to pick a card. They must write the number that is picked into one of their columns. For example, if I picked a 5 I might put that into the hundreds column.

Thousands	Hundreds	Tens	Units
	5		

Once a number is put into a column it cannot be moved. Then put the card back face down onto the table.

3. Repeat this until all of the players have filled all of their columns. The player that has made the highest number wins and gets 10 points. Play the game as many times as you want to!

Variations: use more columns up to one million and down to one hundredth. Instead of trying to make the biggest number you can, make the winning number the smallest you can make.

The more you play maths games, the better you will get at maths.

Just one more game of 'Place Value' and I should be clever enough to apply for the job of Professor of Difficult Mathematics at Oxford.

Glossary

addition – this *operation* combines numbers together by adding one to another to make other numbers (usually bigger). We use the *symbol* + and that means 'plus' or 'add'.

algebra – this is maths with missing bits, sometimes empty boxes, sometimes letters e.g. $3 + M = 4$.

brackets – mathematicians have rules about the order in which we work out parts of a sum or *equation*. In this equation $(6 + 4)$ x $2 - 2 =$ we have to do the brackets first, then any multiplication and division, then any addition and subtraction.

billion – in Europe this is usually one million million with 12 zeros, 1,000,000,000,000, but in America a billion is only a thousand million, written with 9 zeros. But beware, sometimes British people use the American meaning.

decimal – a number that needs *place value* columns that are less than one - tenths, hundredths, thousandths.

Hundreds	Tens	Units	•	Tenths	Hundredths	Thousandths
			•			

denominator – the number on the bottom of a *fraction* which tells you how many parts the whole is split into.

difference between – see subtraction.

divide – this is the opposite of *multiplication* and is about dividing up into equal groups. The symbols are ÷ or one number over the other e.g.

$$\frac{15}{3} \qquad 3\overline{)15}$$

equation – a number sentence e.g. $6 + 4 = 10$ where both sides of the = symbol balance.

even numbers – these are numbers that divide equally between 2, so 6 is an even number because 6 apples between 2 children means 3 each and none left over. All other numbers are *odd numbers*.

factor – the factors of a number are all the numbers that *divide* into it exactly, without leaving a remainder e.g. 3 is a factor of 15 because $15 ÷ 3$ is 5 or 3×5 is 15.

fraction – two numbers separated by a line like $\frac{2}{3}$ showing how many pieces of a whole you have. See *denominator* and *numerator*.

function machines – in a function machine the numbers that go in are changed by one or more *operations* that are happening inside the machine, so if a machine multiplies by 2, when 6 goes in, 12 comes out.

lots of – see multiply.

mental maths – maths to be done in your head and <u>not</u> using a calculator!!!

million – a thousand thousand, written with 6 zeros, 1,000,000.

multiple – a number that is in another number's times table e.g. 20 is a multiple of 4 because five 4s are 20.

multiplied/multiply – times tables using the symbols x to make 'lots of' or equal groups of numbers e.g. 3 lots of 4 makes 12 (3 x 4 = 12).

negative numbers – numbers that go below zero as on a number line or a thermometer.

number line – a useful picture to have in your head when calculating.

number sequences – see patterns.

numerator – the number on the top of a fraction which shows you how many fractions you have.

odd numbers – numbers that have one left over when you divide them by 2, so 7 is an odd number because 7 divided by 2 is 3 and one left over. Other numbers are *even*.

operations – there are four basic operations, +, –, x, and ÷.

patterns – a repeated sequence of numbers or shapes e.g.

Number patterns are very important in calculating e.g. 23 + 10 = 33, 33 + 10 = 43.

percentage – an amount that is out of 100 using the symbol %.

perfect numbers – a number that is the sum of its factors e.g. 6 is a perfect number because 1 + 2 + 3 = 6, where 1 and 2 and 3 are the factors of 6.

GLOSSARY

place value – that part of maths that deals with putting numbers into columns where the columns have different values. We usually use groups of 10 so that each column going up is ten times bigger than the one before. Zero is important in place value for showing where columns are empty e.g.

Hundreds	Tens	Units
		3

This means 3.

Hundreds	Tens	Units
	3	0

This means 3 tens or 30.

Hundreds	Tens	Units
3	0	0

This means 3 lots of a hundred or 300.

(See also *decimals*.)

prime number – a number that can only be divided by 1 and itself without leaving a remainder. Another way to think of this is that the only factors a prime number has are 1 and itself e.g. 19.

product – the number when two or more numbers are *multiplied* together e.g. 2 x 3 has the product of 6.

remainder – the bit left over after a division e.g. 7 divided by 2 is 3 remainder 1.

share equally – see divide.

square number – a number that is made from a number multiplied by itself once e.g. 3 x 3 = 9 so 9 is a square number.

subtraction – this *operation* is used to take one number away from another and includes finding the difference between two numbers. Other words include 'less than', 'more than', 'take away'.

symbols – mathematicians use many signs to stand for something, so + means add and x means 'times' or 'multiply' and sometimes a letter such as M can be used for a missing number.

tens and units – we always group numbers in tens in our number system so a number such as 25 means 2 lots of ten and 5 ones or units. See *place value*.

times – *multiplying* two or more numbers together.

Answers

Adding and Subtracting
page 7
36 + 10 = 46
74 – 10 = 64
page 8
1. 47, 57, 67, 77, 87, 97
page 9
2. 23
3. 49
4. 77
5. 99
6. 86
page 10
1. 375
2. 3,244
3. 56,799
4. 123,456,799
page 11
1. 32
2. 61
3. 76
4. 98
page 13
1. 66
2. 56
3. 86
4. 96
5. 37
6. 39
7. 41. (37, 39, 41, 43, 45)
page 14
1. 19
2. 80
3. 47
4. 34
5. 42
6. 63
page 15
1. 180
2. 1,000
3. 100
4. 130
5. 903
6. 170
7. 16,000
page 17
1. 26
2. 37
page 18
Basic MOT
1. 18 and check with
   18 – 5 = 13

2. 27 and check with
   27 – 6 = 21
Advanced MOT
1. 76
2. 90
3. 85

Making Adding and Subtracting Even Easier
page 21
1. 22
2. 40
3. 200
4. 60
5. 30
6. 48
7. 32
8. 400
9. 50
10. 90
page 22
1. 23
2. 25
3. 43
4. 203
5. 90
6. 41
7. 49
8. 34
page 29
6 + 6 = 3 + 9
44 – 1 = 41 + 2
page 30
16 ÷ 4 = 2 + 2
12 x 12 = (10 x 11) + 34
page 33
1. 8
2. 6,666
page 35
1. 80   2. 130   3. 460
4. 500 5. 1,000 6. 1,200
page 36
1. almost 200, actually 199
2. almost double 80,
   actually 159
3. around 200 more than
   234, actually 439
4. these numbers are so
   close the answer must be
   very small, actually 2
page 39
1. 45
2. 76

3. 94
4. 560
5. 357
6. 639
7. 120
8. 359
9. 1,001
10. 301
page 42
672 – 383 = 289
page 43
Colin owes his mum £20.
page 44
1. £14
2. £4
3. – 2
4. – 3
5. – 3

Multiplying and Dividing
page 47
1. 7 x 2 or 2 x 7
2. 11 x 3 or 3 x 11
To multiply a number by ten
thousand add 4 zeros:
3. 30,000
To multiply a number by a
hundred thousand add 5
zeros:
4. 800,000
5. 70
6. 50
7. 1,400
8. 78,000
page 49
1. 3, 6, 9
2. 4, 8, 12
page 57
1. 66
2. 112
3. 158
4. 18
5. 17
6. 16
7. 25
8. 56
9. 18, 24, 30, 36
10. 12
11. 21
12. 12
13. 6
14. 48
15. 36

137

ANSWERS

16. 1,000
17. 6 bits of ribbon and 10 cm left over
18. 77
19. 9
20. 8
21. 31

page 58
22. 1 and 24, 2 and 12, 3 and 8, 4 and 6
23. 9
24. 61
25. no
26. 30
27. 5
28. 6
29. 7 x 9 = 63, 9 x 7 = 63, $\frac{63}{9}$ = 7, $\frac{63}{7}$ = 9
30. yes
1. 3 x 4 = 12
   4 x 3 = 12
   12 ÷ 4 = 3
   12 ÷ 3 = 4
2. 6 x 7 = 42
   7 x 6 = 42
   42 ÷ 6 = 7
   42 ÷ 7 = 6
3. 3 x 9 = 27
   9 x 3 = 27
   27 ÷ 3 = 9
   27 ÷ 9 = 3

page 60
3. 40,000

page 61
1. 48
2. 60
3. 72, 84, 96, 108, 120, 132, 144

Messing about with Numbers
page 64
1. 7
2. 2
3. 9
4. 39
5. 199

page 65
1. 36, 45, 54, 63
2. no

page 66
3. 45, add 4 + 5 = 9 54, add 5 + 4 = 9 etc
4. 9, 11, 13 the odd numbers.

Watch Puzzle

page 68
1. 1 by 24, 2 by 12, 3 by 8, 4 by 6. That is 4 different ones.
2. lots of possible numbers e.g. 12, 32, 48, 96, 108
3. 48

page 69
4. 17, 19, 23, 29, 31. If your list goes further than our answers, ask an adult to check your work.
5. yes

page 70
Basic MOT
1. 28
2. 496 and 8,128
Fizz in this Quiz
1. 7 and 7
2. 6 and 10
3. 3 and 19
4. 15 and 3
5. 12 and 12
6. 25 and 3

page 71
Be Great when you Estimate
1. +
2. x
3. ÷
4. –

page 72
Frustrating Challenge
0. 4 – 3 – 2 + 1
1. 1 x 2 + 3 – 4
2. 1 + 2 + 3 – 4
3. 4 + 2 – (1 x 3)
4. 1 + 2 – 3 + 4
5. 4 + 3 – (2 x 1)
6. 1 – 2 + 3 + 4 or 1 + 3 – 2 + 4
7. (4 x 3) ÷ 2 + 1
8. 4 + 3 + 2 – 1
9. 1 x 2 + 3 + 4
10. 1 + 2 + 3 + 4
11. (4 x 3) – 2 + 1
12. (4 x 2) + 3 + 1

13. (4 + 3) x 2 – 1
14. (4 + 3) x 2 x 1
15. (4 x 3) + 2 + 1
16. (4 x 2) x (3 – 1)
17. (4 + 2) x 3 – 1
18. (4 + 2) x (3 x 1)
19. (4 + 2) x 3 + 1
20. 1 x (2 + 3) x 4
Really Frustrating Challenge
two possible answers are
123 + 45 – 67 + 8 – 9 = 100
and 12 + 3 – 4 + 5 + 67 + 8 + 9 = 100

Fractions
page 76
1. 3
2. 5
3. 10
4. 19
5. 13
6. 30
7. $\frac{1}{3}$
8. $\frac{1}{2}$
9. $\frac{1}{6}$
10. $\frac{1}{2}$
11. $\frac{1}{3}$
12. $\frac{1}{3}$

page 77

page 79
pair up $\frac{1}{3}$ with $\frac{2}{6}$
pair up $\frac{2}{8}$ with $\frac{1}{4}$
pair up $\frac{4}{8}$ with $\frac{1}{2}$
pair up $\frac{1}{2}$ with $\frac{3}{6}$

page 82
1. 6
2. 6
3. 20
4. 20

page 83
1. 10
2. 10

138

3. 15
4. 49
5. 2
6. 80
True or False
1. T
2. T
3. F
4. T
5. F
6. T

Place Value
page 88
1, 2, 3:

Hundred thousands	Ten thousands	Thousands	Hundreds	Tens	Units
	1	0	6	4	2

Hundred thousands	Ten thousands	Thousands	Hundreds	Tens	Units
2	2	7	8	1	5

Hundred thousands	Ten thousands	Thousands	Hundreds	Tens	Units
1		5	0	0	4

page 91
1. 940
2. 94
3. 590
4. 59
Place Value MOT
1. four hundred thousand
2. four million
3. one million, two hundred and thirty-four thousand, five hundred and sixty-seven
4. one thousand, three hundred and nine
5. one thousand and four
6. 6 thousand
page 92
7. 6 tens
8. 6 units
9. I'd rather have (a) because it is two hundred, a hundred times more than (b) which is £2
10. 620
11. 65
12. 90

Decimals
page 97
1. 0.3
2. 0.4

3. 0.5
4. 0.6
page 98
Guessable Decimals!
1. 15.3
2. 28.1
3. 31.9
4. 45.8
Mega Tricky Guessable Decimals!
1. 147.5
2. 176.2
3. 1,563.9
4. 17,653.7
page 101
1. £876,543.21
2. 34,567.89 m
3. 12,345,678.90 m
4. £98,700.03
5. £67
6. 8,000 m
page 103
Guzzle at this Puzzle
1. 938.0 or 938
2. 93.8
3. 4.51
4. 45.1
5. 95,620.9
6. 9,562.09
It's Rude To Point
1. £7.00
2. £8.50
3.

Hundreds	Tens	Units	•	Tenths	Hundredths
			•		
			•		

4. 0.5
5. 3.4
It's Extremely Rude To Point
1. seven point nine eight
2. 8
3. 9
4. 7
5. 839.0 or 839
Challenge

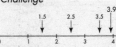

Calculators
page 106
1. 4
2. 579
3. 666
4. 14,400

5. 25,600
6. 37
7. 777
8. 1,111
9. 2.08
10. 0.25
page 111
1. 16 and 25
2. 100
3. yes
page 113
1. 1 x 2 x 3
2. 5 x 6 x 7 = 210
3. 7 x 8 x 9 = 504
4. 9 x 10 x 11 = 990

Percentages
page 116
1. $\frac{48}{100}$ 48%

2. $\frac{99}{100}$ 99%

3. $\frac{65}{100}$ 65%

4. $\frac{50}{100}$ 50%

page 120
1. £9
2. £15
3. £30
4. £40
page 123
1. 20
2. 90
3. 10.8
4. 21

Colin Jets off on Holiday
page 126
1. He could take any one of them or b and c, or a and e.
2. $34
3. 172 Fr.
4. 13p for one, 26p for two
5. 3,000 miles
page 127
6. 810 Fr.
7. £12 is $20.40 and so selling at $10 it is much cheaper in America.
8. It is $10 less $1.50 so it costs $8.50

139

Index